Teaching Cues for Sport Skills

Teaching Cues
for Sport Skills

Hilda Ann Fronske
Utah State University

Allyn and Bacon
Boston • London • Toronto • Sydney • Tokyo • Singapore

Senior Editor: Suzy Spivey
Editorial Assistant: Amy Braddock
Composition and Prepress Buyer: Linda Cox
Manufacturing Buyer: Suzanne Lareau
Cover Administrator: Suzanne Harbison
Production Administrator: Deborah Brown
Editorial-Production Service: P. M. Gordon Associates, Inc.

Copyright © 1997 by Allyn and Bacon
A Viacom Company
160 Gould Street
Needham Heights, MA 02194

Internet: www.abacon.com
America Online: keyword: College Online

Library of Congress Cataloging-in-Publication Data

Fronske, Hilda Ann.
    Teaching cues for sport skills / Hilda Ann Fronske.
        p. cm.
    Includes bibliographical references and index.
    ISBN 0–205–18610–6
    1. Sports—Study and teaching.   2. Coaching (Athletics)
I. Title.
GV361.F66   1996
796′.07—dc21   96–48862
                                           CIP

Printed in the United States of America
10 9 8 7 6 5 4   01 00 99

To Carl McGown, my mentor, and to my kindred spirit Patsy Bradfield, her husband Lyle, and their four sons Tim, Tom, Todd, and Jason

Contents

Preface

Cues will provide "hooks" on which to hang memories of skill instruction. We find that our students can tell us many of the cues they receive in their activity classes years after completing the class.

—Fronske & McGown, 1992

What goals do you have for yourself as a teacher? What goals do you have for your students? If you want to be the most effective teacher you can be, and if you want your students to be able to learn quickly, demonstrate correctly, and *remember* motor skills, then this book is for you! The contents will increase your teaching vocabulary, causing you to become a more effective teacher.

A cue is a short, catchy phrase that calls the learner's attention to key components of a skill. It projects a clear description into the mind's eye of the student, sometimes by relating the skill to be learned to common or unrelated knowledge.

Recent research has shown that coaches and teachers who use cues when teaching motor skills are more effective than those who do not use them. However, developing cues for a variety of sports is difficult and extremely time-consuming. I have written this book to help place teachers and coaches on the cutting edge of more effective teaching and to save them a great deal of time.

Teaching Cues for Sport Skills is designed to provide verbal and visual teaching cues, alternate teaching cues, and common errors for a wide variety of sports. The cues are presented in a teaching progression. For each specific skill and sport, I have consulted experts to develop the best possible cues for that sport.

Chapter 1 is representative of the strategies and methods included in this book. This introductory chapter presents a definition of teaching cues, the benefits of using cues, the use of cues in demonstrations, rules to follow when using cues, the use of cues as a method for analyzing motor skills, guidelines for incorporating cues, using cues to strengthen correct performance, and ways for instructors and peers to correct errors in technique by using cues. Chapter 1 also shows that cues need to be given in a supportive climate and that cues may be used to motivate students to develop and refine skills. It also provides a successful teaching model and guidelines for cue making, and explains the use of cues in evaluating student performance for grading.

Instructors can use correct teaching methods by incorporating the cues into the teaching process. The book's emphasis on practical application is designed to help instructors and coaches choose and refine a vocabulary of teaching cues.

The usefulness of this book lies in its comprehensive coverage of the cues and common errors for a variety of sport skills. Included in each chapter is a brief introduction, skills listed with cues, teaching tips, equipment tips, and innovative teaching ideas. A section called FYI (for your information) provides access to current phone numbers, fax numbers, and addresses where updated information and teaching materials regarding the specific sport can be obtained. Precise analytic illustrations accompany the tables of visual or verbal teaching cues, alternate teaching cues, and common errors. Chapters 2 through 26 provide educators with a complete selection of teaching cues and their components for the following sports: archery, badminton, baseball, basketball, bowling, cross-country running, cycling (mountain biking and road biking), field hockey, flag football, floor hockey, golf, lacrosse, Pickle-Ball, racquetball, skiing (cross-country), soccer, softball, swimming, team handball, tennis, track and field, tumbling, ultimate Frisbee, volleyball, and weight lifting.

Cues work! Gold medalists and successful teams attest to their usefulness.

Acknowledgments

I would like to express my sincere appreciation to Carl McGown for sharing his knowledge and expertise with me; to Robert P. Pangrazi and Connie Blakemore for seeing the vision of the book; to Joyce Harrison for her patience, intellect, and wisdom; to Ann Smith for believing in me and encouraging me to write; to Robert P. Pangrazi, *Strategies*, and the *Journal of Physical Education, Recreation, and Dance* for publishing my articles; and to Suzy Spivey, Lisa Davidson, and Joan Saidel for their incredible support and editing ideas for the book.

Thanks to Pat Bradfield for the countless hours she spent reviewing the manuscript and encouraging me to finish. Special thanks go to Gwen Haws; Linda Keith, university editor, Utah State University, and Becky Smith for editing the manuscript; to Colonel Byron Hukee for generously giving of his time to format the manuscript; and to Tami Oram and Lisa Klarich for the many hours they spent entering the data on the computer. Kudos to Joey Taylor for his incredible talent and willingness to work tirelessly to meet the deadlines. This book will be richer because of his artistic drawing. Best wishes to him as he pursues his creative artistic endeavors. To Bud Kirn for his artistic skill in designing the rough-draft illustrations. To Robyn Christiansen, ALF Engen Ski School, Alta, Utah. A very special thank you goes to my father and mother, Robert Martin Fronske and Maire Therese Fronske, who taught me to work hard, and to my grandfather, Martin George Fronske, who was my example and inspired me to pursue my education.

In addition, I would like to acknowledge and thank the following reviewers for their constructive suggestions and comments throughout the development of the manuscript.

Larry M. Albertson
University of Wisconsin—River Falls

Dr. June I. Decker
Western New Mexico University

Dr. Connie Fox
Northern Illinois University

Linda Griffin
University of Massachusetts/Amherst

Linda English Haverstock
Murray State University

Margaret Pentecost
University of Louisville

SPORT CONSULTANTS

I wish to thank all of the sport consultants who generously shared their time, knowledge, and expertise in their specific sport with me.

Archery

Joyce Harrison, associate dean
Brigham Young University, Provo, Utah

Derek Lindley, archery manager
Al's Sporting Goods, Logan, Utah

Badminton

Gord Smith
Badminton Canada, Gloucester, Ontario, Canada

Richard Jones
Brigham Young University, Provo, Utah

Baseball

Justin Jensen, associate scout for Milwaukee Brewers
Rocky Mountain School of Baseball, Logan, Utah

Jonathan Howell
Department of Health, Physical Education, and Recreation, Utah State University, Logan, Utah

Basketball

Ann Asbell, activity specialist
Department of Exercise and Sport Science, Oregon State University, Corvallis, Oregon

Karen Logan, former basketball pro
Logan, Utah

Bowling

Richard Jones, professor in pedagogy and sports
Brigham Young University, Provo, Utah

Cross-Country Running

Patrick Shane, head women's cross-country/distance coach
Brigham Young University, Provo, Utah

Cycling—Mountain Biking

Jeff Keller
Sunrise Cycle, Logan, Utah

Steven G. Gudmundson, graduate student
Utah State University, Logan, Utah

Cycling—Road Biking

Jeff Keller
Sunrise Cycle, Logan, Utah

Steven G. Gudmundson, graduate student
Utah State University, Logan, Utah

Field Hockey

Laura Darling
United States Field Hockey Association, Colorado, Springs, Colorado

Katie Harris and Deanie Stetson
Falmouth High School, Falmouth, Maine

Flag Football

Art Erickson, player and coach
Utah State University, Logan, Utah

Floor Hockey

Gianni F. Maddalozzo
Department of Exercise and Sport Science, Oregon State University, Corvallis, Oregon

Golf

Brett Wayment, assistant professional
Logan Country Club, Logan, Utah

Robert Fronske, amateur golf player
Tempe, Arizona

Pickle-Ball

Doug Smith, general manager
Pickle-Ball, Inc., Seattle, Washington

Racquetball

Jim Hiser
American Amateur Racquetball Association, Colorado Springs, Colorado

Susan Hill, graduate student
Health Department,
    Southern Illinois University,
    Carbondale, Illinois

Skiing, Cross-Country

Tim Trezise
Department of Health, Physical
    Education, and Recreation, Utah
    State University, Logan, Utah

Soccer

Chris Agnello, men's soccer coach
Department of Exercise and Sport
    Science, University of Utah, Salt Lake
    City, Utah

Charles Dudschus
Department of Health, Physical
    Education, and Recreation, Utah
    State University, Logan

Jin Wang, men's soccer coach
Department of Health, Physical
    Education, and Athletics, Valdosta
    State University, Valdosta, Georgia

Softball

Lloydene Searle, head women's fast-
    pitch softball coach
Utah State University, Logan, Utah

Ann A. Schulz
Sandridge Junior High School, Layton,
    Utah

Swimming

Lisa Klarich and Steven Dunn
Department of Health, Physical
    Education, and Recreation, Utah
    State University, Logan, Utah

Team Handball

Mary Phyl Dwight, cochair, Coaching
    and Methods Committee
United States Team Handball
    Federation, Kansas City, Missouri

Reita Clanton, assistant coach for
    Women Team Handball Team
Atlanta, Georgia

Tennis

Janet Carey, tennis pro
Neversink, New York

Dan Clifton, tennis instructor
Campus recreation instructional
    program, Utah State University,
    Logan, Utah

Steven Dunn, Rolayne Wilson, and Clay
    Stevens
Utah State University, Logan, Utah

Track and Field

Curtis Collier, track technician
Utah State University, Logan

Tumbling

Tana Davis and Kim Autenrieb
Ten-O-Gymnastics Academy, Logan,
    Utah

Ultimate Frisbee

Ann Asbell, activity specialist
Department of Exercise and Sport
    Science, Oregon State University,
    Corvallis, Oregon

Janenne Graff, player/coach
Ultimate Frisbee Club, Utah State
    University, Logan, Utah

Volleyball

Carl McGown
Department of Physical Education,
    Brigham Young University, Provo,
    Utah

Weight Lifting

Art Erickson and Don Gowans
Department of Health, Physical
    Education, and Recreation, Utah
    State University, Logan, Utah

Nicole Anastasia McKenzie
North Dakota State University, Fargo,
    North Dakota

Chapter 1

What Are Teaching Cues?

A cue is defined as a guiding suggestion, or a stimulus that excites the imagination to action. Cues are short, catchy phrases that call the student's attention to key components of a skill. A cue projects a clear description of a skill component into the mind's eye of the student (Christiansen, personal interview, 1995).

Cues may be verbal in nature, serving as a short reminder of more complete information presented about a skill. A cue developed around rich visual imagery or related to the student's previous experience will remain in cognition much longer than a lengthy dissertation on the fine points of technique. A mind cluttered with many technical concepts cannot direct the muscles to achieve flawless coordination. At best, a mind concentrating on one visual or kinesthetic prompt may direct that one body part to obey the command (Christiansen, personal interview, 1995). For example, a verbal cue for shooting-hand preparation in a set shot is "palm up." Phrases may also be more visual in nature with the intent of creating a picture in the learner's mind that results in correct skill performance. The "palm up" cue could be followed by "like holding a waiter's tray." "Make an hourglass or keyhole shape with your arms" when performing the butterfly stroke or "Scrape the sides of the bowl with your hands" when performing the breaststroke arm action are other examples of prompts that provide a rich visual image for students to identify the skill component. By picturing these familiar patterns, students are able to develop correct skill patterns and, if they begin to show poorer form, a cue serves as a quick reminder of proper form. Rule and strategy cues, although slightly longer than skill cues, are designed to be quick reminders for students to focus on when they are learning a rule or strategy.

Too often when teaching sport skills, the teacher overloads the student with too much information and technical jargon that make little sense to the student. Motor learning specialists have long noted that the simpler the instruction, the easier it is for students to concentrate on the skill at hand. The KISS principle, "Keep it simple, stupid," is applied.

WHAT ARE THE BENEFITS OF USING TEACHING CUES?

Physical education teachers have students for only short periods of time during the week. It is imperative that this time be utilized to the fullest. The use of short, accurate, qualitative teaching cues can save the teacher hours and eliminate many complications. Research indicates that accurate, qualitative cues, appropriate numbers of cues, and the use of visual demonstrations with verbal explanations together seem to produce greater performance gains of skill development in classes (Rink, 1993). The cues in this book have been developed by experts to help teachers give accurate, qualitative cues regarding a specific sport skill. These cues *work*!

- Cues enhance the learner's memory (Figure 1.1).
- Cues compress information and reduce words.
- Cues encourage focus on one specific component of a skill.
- Cues help teachers and students analyze a skill performance by helping them focus on a particular component of the skill.
- Cues strengthen correct performance.
- Cues help teachers give positive, corrective feedback.
- Cues help peers give positive, corrective feedback.
- Cues motivate students to develop and refine skills (Christina & Corcos, 1988; McGown, unpublished lecture notes, 1988).

Robyn Christiansen (personal interview, 1995) makes this statement about teaching cues for skiing: "A cue is defined as a guiding suggestion, or a stimulus that excites to action. In the realm of teaching snow skiing, cues are frequently used to simplify and enhance students' learning experience." Skiing requires difficult physical and mental concepts translated into movement patterns that allow the free-flowing grace of the expert skier.

CUES USED IN CONJUNCTION WITH A DEMONSTRATION

Cues used with a demonstration help students to develop a strong visual image of the skill. When demonstrating a skill, the teacher focuses the student's attention on one spe-

FIGURE 1.1 Cues Enhance Memory.

cific component of the skill through the use of a good verbal or visual cue. To avoid confusing the student, it is important to keep verbalization to a minimum. For example, having students mimic tying a knot with their hands as they learn the sidestroke gives them a familiar picture upon which to base their skill performance when they hear and see the phrase "tie a knot" as they swim. By picturing the correct pattern, they are able to develop the correct sidestroke arm patterns. If they begin to show improper form, a cue, a demonstration, or both serve as quick reminders of proper form.

RULES TO FOLLOW WHEN USING CUES

Research in motor learning indicates that students can learn only a limited amount of new material. Giving students too much information or progressing to new information before students have grasped a concept may hinder the learning process (Figure 1.2). Too much information is worse than providing no information at all.

For each component of a skill, practice the whole skill, but focus on each part in turn. No more than one or two cues at a time should be given to students. Following the acquisition of the motor pattern (i.e., "heart shape" with hands for swimming the breaststroke) targeted by the first cue, teachers then move to the next phase of the motor skill.

Additional cues should build on the previously learned skills, with no more than three to five cues for each teaching episode. Students need short bits of information they can quickly apply to their skill.

FIGURE 1.2 Information Overload.

CUES HELP INSTRUCTORS ANALYZE A SKILL

Poor physical education teachers tend to analyze skills excessively and tell all they know (Lockhart, 1966). Teachers might consider incorporating effective teaching cues in the instructional process to avoid these pitfalls. Cues are short and to the point, and they turn the analysis process toward giving specific feedback.

Teaching cues, such as those presented in this text, not only provide students with a valuable aid to accompany demonstrations but also aid the teacher in focusing on correct skill performances so that appropriate feedback can be given. Incorporating cues in the teaching process makes it possible for teachers to identify major errors quickly. For example, when students are performing the forehand stroke in tennis and the instructor's cue is "Racquet head needs to finish on edge," it is easily determined if the racquet head is "on edge" at the end of the stroke.

GUIDELINES FOR INCORPORATION OF CUES

Once the teacher decides to use teaching cues as part of the instruction process, several guidelines for their use are helpful.

1. Formulate and prioritize cues. The teacher must decide what a performer should concentrate on first, then second, then third to execute a skill correctly.
2. Keep individual cues and total cue lists compact and concise. Usually three effective cues are sufficient.
3. Give only one cue at a time.

Christina and Corcos (1988, pp. 99–102) have added the following suggestions for correcting errors based on cue presentation:

1. Decide if error needs correction. Change technique only if a performer is not fundamentally sound, if changing will improve performance, or if performance is not safe.
2. Determine the cause of incorrect cue execution and how to correct the error. The causes may change the feedback focus.
   a. Forgetfulness
   b. Lack of understanding
   c. Lack of prerequisite skill
   d. Physical disability
   e. Poor physical capability
   f. Fear
3. Correct one error at a time. Identify and eliminate the critical error. This may be the earliest in the sequence.
4. Provide useful feedback for the student. The message should be easily understood.
5. Include positive encouragement and present it at the appropriate time.

USING CUES TO STRENGTHEN CORRECT PERFORMANCE

A critical component for teachers and students is to identify the parts of the skill that are being performed correctly. The teacher can have the students work in groups in which they can be assigned to analyze and give feedback for one specific cue. For example, if the following cues for throwing a ball are used: 1) "Take the ball straight down and graze your shorts," 2) "Stretch your arm way back," and 3) "Make an L," responses may include 1) "Hey, I liked the way you brought your arm down and grazed your shorts. That action will give you more distance"; or 2) "Wow! Way to stretch that arm back; that was a great stretch. That stretch looks like Barry Bonds or Dale Murphy"; or 3) "Way to make an L shape with your arm. You're keeping the ball away from your head like we need to." This type of feedback will increase the tendency of the student to repeat the response in the near future and also strengthen the correct response (Fronske, Abendroth-Smith, & Blakemore, in press).

The preceding responses include reasons why the students should perform the particular cue. If you stretch your arm way back, you will throw the ball farther and with more power. It is important to provide a reason why one needs to perform a particular cue accurately.

INSTRUCTORS CORRECT ERRORS IN TECHNIQUE BY USING CUES

"Coach, how can I go over the hurdles faster?" "How do I improve my sprint time?" "What is the best way to exchange the baton?" These are questions students might ask about track skills. Is the teacher ready to answer these questions without criticizing or giving the learner too much information (Fronske, Collier, & Orr, 1993)?

The teacher's challenge is to identify the cause of the problem and look for solutions rather than judge or criticize. The effective use of cues avoids judgment and criticism. By sandwiching feedback, a teacher can use cues to correct errors constructively (Docheff, 1990) (Figure 1.3). Cues help the teacher identify the problem and provide accurate feedback to the student. An example of sandwiching would be, "Stacie, I really liked how you made a 'banana shape' when performing the long jump; this time, make sure you work on the 'jackknife position' when you land. But, way to make the banana shape."

FIGURE 1.3 Sandwich Feedback.

FIGURE 1.4   Peer Giving Feedback.

STUDENTS/PEERS CORRECT ERRORS IN TECHNIQUE BY USING CUES

When students are provided with correct teaching cues, they can help the teacher give feedback to their peers. This can be done by pairing students up and having each one observe a partner's performance. For example, if the cue given on throwing is "Stand sideways and take a long step toward the target," the student can watch her partner, determine if she is standing sideways, and analyze the foot action. If her partner steps too high or takes a short step but is standing sideways, she can provide her partner with the following feedback: "Hey, Stacie, you stood sideways; now remember to take a longer step with your foot toward the target." This feedback emphasizes the student's correct performance, notifies her of her error, and suggests a specific way to correct the error. The use of cues provides a more positive method for interaction. Students are receptive to peer feedback (see Figure 1.4).

CUES NEED TO BE GIVEN IN A SUPPORTIVE CLIMATE

Teachers need to establish a framework of support in order to successfully implement teaching cues. Students need to feel safe in order to reach out and try new behaviors. Creating a supportive climate creates a safe learning environment for students. The supportive climate is partly a result of positive, clear verbal cues and reinforcing phrases. It is also a result of a safe nonverbal physical environment.

Nonverbal aspects that accompany verbal cues also communicate to students. A teacher who says "nice" accompanied by a harsh tone of voice and disapproving facial expressions communicates "bad dive." The way teachers present cues, the tones of their voices, their body language, touch, or dress (such as a swim teacher not in a swimming suit) can enhance or detract from a positive environment.

According to J. D. Lawther (1968), a teacher should "use constructive guidance rather than faultfinding in teaching the beginner. The free-flowing smoothness of automatic skill does not develop in a tense situation. The beginner needs normal tonus of his functioning musculature and relaxation in the antagonists."

Great teachers and coaches are skillful at giving the most appropriate cue at the appropriate time, using verbal or nonverbal signals. Combining verbal cues and positive nonverbal cues becomes a powerful tool for the teacher or coach to give feedback (Fronske & Birch, 1995).

When teachers provide a supportive climate, students feel comfortable and are motivated to explore and learn a variety of sports (see Figure 1.5).

USING CUES TO MOTIVATE STUDENTS TO DEVELOP AND REFINE SKILLS

Recent research has found that students who receive cues appear to be more motivated to improve their performance than students who do not receive verbal cues. Their self-confidence seems to increase steadily with improved skill ability, and they work hard to improve each day. Students without cues appear to become frustrated and bored and have a difficult time staying on task (Fronske, Abendroth-Smith, & Blakemore, in press).

Cues arouse students to direct their efforts toward improving their performance and provide a foundation for setting goals. When students feel the success of learning one cue at a time, other cues can be introduced without intimidation until the students become proficient at the complete skill component. Mastering one cue at a time gives students very specific goals to work for. Providing a few alternate cues allows students to choose one and work at their own pace. Cues help all students experience success with sport skills.

FIGURE 1.5   Create a Supportive Climate.

A SUCCESSFUL TEACHING MODEL

How does a teacher teach a motor skill correctly? What is a correct and successful teaching model? How do teaching cues fit in this model? The following list includes components of a good teaching model and ways to implement cues (Christina & Corcos, 1988; McGown, 1988).

1. First, get the student's attention! Enthusiasm from the teacher motivates the student to want to perform the skill. Make sure the student pays attention to the instructions.
2. Organize the group so everyone can see and hear the introduction, objective, and demonstration.
3. State your objective of the lesson by describing what is to be learned and why it is important. This description should lead to the demonstration that follows. Your objective should be brief, simple, and direct.
4. Preassess the students by asking how many of them know how to perform the skill, or ask the students to perform the skill if the skill is relatively safe (Figure 1.6).
5. Demonstrate the entire skill three to five times. Show the skill from front, side, and back angles. Demonstrations should be performed in the same direction as they would appear in a game situation. The students should be able to see a correct demonstration of the skill. Remember a picture is worth a thousand words when learning a sport skill.
6. After the demonstrations, have the learners practice the skill. The teacher then has time to assess each player's proficiency.
7. Demonstrate the entire skill, adding one or two teaching cues, and direct the student's attention to the specific area of focus as outlined by the cue words.
8. Have students practice the skill; teachers then give feedback with cue words used in the demonstration. Instruct small groups one by one, down a line. If another demonstration is needed, then come back to the last student instructed and continue on down the line until all students have received proper instruction.
9. Provide additional demonstrations and new cues when students have mastered previous cues.

FIGURE 1.6 Preassess the Student's Ability.

10. Provide cues and demonstrations for gamelike drills, modified games, strategies, rules, scoring, and skill tests. Use scoring, targets, and goals in your gamelike drills.
11. Review or demonstrate the cues to close the lesson. Have a student who learned the skill be the demonstrator. Provide the students with an opportunity to ask questions.

GUIDELINES TO CUE MAKING

Here are some suggestions for designing cues. These are some ideas to help create your own (Blakemore, 1995).

1. Go to the sources—skill books, skill videos, workshops, experts, and the like—to make sure the cue is accurate.
2. Condense the skill analysis or description to a few effective words. Find the catchy words, metaphors, short phrases, choice words in the resources. Avoid long sentences.
3. Properly sequence the cues.
4. Find what is critical to the task—three to five cues. Decide which is the most important cue for the skill, then the second, third, and so on. For example, see throwing and batting cues.
5. Keep the cues few in number: three to five.
6. Design the cues for the appropriate age and learning stage.
7. Cut pictures out of a sports section in a newspaper or a sport magazine, or use a sports photograph of a student-athlete in your class; type one to three cues, and place the typed cues directly on the pictures and copy. Display these pictures in gyms, locker rooms, and recreation centers and at athletic events (Figure 1.7).

FIGURE 1.7 Analysis of Sports Action Pictures Using Cues.

USING CUES TO EVALUATE STUDENT PERFORMANCES FOR GRADING

Physical education teachers have a new tool to evaluate and grade students. A teacher can evaluate the students specifically on the cues taught. The students know specific components of the skill they need to work on and how they will be evaluated. This approach gives students an opportunity to practice the important cues.

Teachers can design a three-point checklist. This is an easy way to grade and a method to eliminate subjective grading by the teacher. The teacher focuses on specific cues. For example, in tennis a three-point checklist for the forehand stroke and volley stroke might include:

Forehand Stroke

1. Pivot and step, ball contact made even at left hip
2. Firm wrist or arm in cast
3. Finish on edge

Volley Stroke

1. Step and punch (racquet never goes behind front shoulder)
2. Firm wrist, firm grip
3. Hand below ball

Preservice teachers can also use this tool to evaluate peers in their skill analysis classes and method classes. They can choose the three best cues for a skill, teach the cues, and then evaluate their peers on the cues. No more than three cues should be used to evaluate students, to concur with Rink's systematic observation (Darst, Zakrajsek, & Mancini, 1989), "An effective teacher uses between 1–3 cues." We want to avoid overloading the students' information-processing centers. The key here is to choose the best three cues to teach a skill and emphasize those three cues for evaluation purposes.

CONCLUSION

Teaching skill techniques using proper cues is a methodology that should be impressed upon preservice teachers as well as experienced practitioners. Teachers should gain skill in creating and incorporating the best cues for their own students. Developing the skill aids the teacher in giving meaningful demonstrations whereby students are able to identify specific actions from the demonstrator. Furthermore, cues offer a method of analyzing and evaluating specific motor skills. They also provide the teacher with corrective feedback. Cues need to be adapted to the age and skill level of the students for their skills to be developed and refined.

Creating a supportive climate helps students feel comfortable and safe and motivates them to reach out and try new behaviors.

Cues provide a vital link for teachers teaching motor skills, rules, and strategies. Teachers who use cues 1) with demonstrations, 2) to analyze skills, drills, and strategies, 3) to strengthen correct performance, 4) to give appropriate corrective feedback, 5) for evaluation purposes, and 6) for motivational purposes eliminate improper instruction while keeping students motivated and on task.

Cues also benefit the students. The brief phrases or words contained in this book will help students remember critical and specific elements of the skill. These metaphors make it easy for students to remember the skill being taught by providing hooks on which to hang memories of skill instruction.

Included in the following chapters are brief introductions, skills listed with cues, teaching tips, equipment tips, teaching ideas, accurate qualitative teaching cues, alternate cues, and common errors for 25 sports.

FYI

For further information, consult the following sources:

Feltz, D. (1982). The effects of age and number of demonstrations on modeling of form performance. *Research Quarterly, 53*, 291–296.

Gallahue, D. L., & Ozmun, J. C. (1995). *Understanding motor development* (3rd ed.). Madison, WI: Brown & Benchmark.

Graham, G., Holt/Hale, S., & Parker, M. (1993). *Children moving: A reflective approach to teaching physical education* (3rd ed.). Mountain View, CA: Mayfield.

Hall, L. T. (1994). *Motor learning lecture notes*. Dubuque, IA: Kendall/Hunt.

Hand, J., & Sidaway, B. (1992, March). Relative frequency of modeling effects on the performance and retention of a motor skill. *Research Quarterly for Exercise and Sport* (Suppl. A), 57–58.

Harrison, J., & Blakemore, C. L. (1992). *Instructional strategies for secondary school physical education* (3rd ed.). Dubuque, IA: Wm. C. Brown.

Kirchner, G., & Fishburne, G. J. (1995). *Physical education for elementary school children*. Dubuque, IA: Brown & Benchmark.

Landers, D. (1975). Observational learning of a motor skill: Temporal spacing of demonstrations and audience presence. *Journal of Motor Behavior, 7*, 281–287.

Martens, R., Burwitz, L., & Zuckerman, J. (1976). Modeling effects on motor performance. *Research Quarterly for Exercise and Sport, 47*, 277–291.

Mood, D., Musker, F., & Rink, J. (1991). *Sports and recreational activities* (10th ed.). St. Louis, MO: Mosby.

Pangrazi, R., & Darst, P. W. (1997). *Dynamic physical education for secondary school students* (3rd ed.). Boston: Allyn & Bacon.

Pangrazi, R., & Dauer, V. (1995). *Dynamic physical education for elementary children* (11th ed.). Boston: Allyn & Bacon.

Pollock, B., & Lee, T. (1992). Effects of the mode's skill level on observational motor learning. *Research Quarterly for Exercise and Sport, 63*(1), 25–29.

Rink, J. (1985). *Teaching physical education for learning*. St. Louis, MO: Times Mirror/Mosby.

Roberton, M. A. (1984). Changing motor patterns during childhood and adolescence. In J. R. Thomas (Ed.), *Motor development during childhood and adolescence* (pp. 48–49). Minneapolis, MN: Burgess.

Sage, G. H. (1984). *Motor learning and control—A neuropsychological approach*. Dubuque, IA: Wm. C. Brown.

FYI

Continued

Schmidt, R. A. (1982). *Motor control and learning*. Champaign, IL: Human Kinetics.

Seaton, D. C., Schmottlach, N., Clayton, I., Leibee, H.C., & Messersmith, L.L. (1983). *Physical education handbook*. Englewood Cliffs, NJ: Prentice-Hall.

Seaton, D. C., Schmottlach, N., McManama, J. L., Clayton, I. A., Leibee, H. C., & Messersmith, L. L. (1992). *Physical education handbook* (11th ed.). Englewood Cliffs, NJ: Prentice-Hall.

Siedentop, D. (1991). *Developing teaching skills in physical education*. Mountain View, CA: Mayfield.

Siedentop, D. (1990). *Introduction to physical education, fitness, and sport*. Mountain View, CA: Mayfield.

Smith, T. L., & Eason, R. L. (1990). Effects of verbal and visual cues on performance of a complex ballistic task. *Perceptual and Motor Skills, 70,* 1163–1168.

Thomas, J. R., Thomas, K. T., Gallagher, J. D. (1993). *Handbook of research on sport psychology: Developmental considerations in skill acquisition*. New York: Macmillan.

Weeks, D., & Finchum, J. (1992, March). A comparison of the contribution of perceptual modeling and knowledge of results to coincident-timing skill acquisition. *Research Quarterly for Exercise and Sport* (Suppl. A), 62.

Weiss, M. (1983). Modeling and motor performance: A developmental perspective. *Research Quarterly, 54,* 190–197.

Werner, P., & Rink, J. (1989). Case studies of teacher effectiveness in second grade physical education. *Journal of Teaching Physical Education, 12*(4), 280–297.

Wiese-Bjornstal, D., & Weiss, M. (1992). Modeling effects on children's form kinematics, performance outcome, and cognitive recognition of a sport skill: An integrated perspective. *Research Quarterly for Exercise and Sport, 63*(3), 67–75.

Yando, R., Seitz, V., & Zigler, E. (1978). *Imitation: A developmental perspective*. New York: Wiley.

Chapter 2

Archery

INTRODUCTION

Are you looking for a new way to have fun or a new sport to add to your curriculum? Archery is one of the oldest sports participated in today. Why is archery still being enjoyed by many? Young and old alike enjoy the challenge of hitting a target. Archery can also be played year-round: indoors during inclement weather and outdoors in the fresh air. Archery provides opportunities for exercise and competition. Those who join archery clubs or leagues can participate with archers their own age. In many high schools and universities, students can join archery teams and perhaps even receive scholarships.

Archery is an inexpensive sport to start. All the beginning archery gear needed costs less than a pair of top athletic shoes. If students are taught the fundamental archery skills, display an interest, and experience success, teachers could then suggest they pursue related sports, which include field archery, bow hunting, and bow fishing.

By providing these archery cues teachers might incorporate archery into their curricula. Consequently, students of all ages can learn a new sport and "be on target for fun" (Parker & Bars, 1994).

SKILLS LISTED WITH CUES

In this chapter we have designed equipment cues for selecting a bow, arrows, arm guard, and finger tab. Cues are given for safety techniques and retrieving arrows from a target. The other cues cover beginning skills for the stance address, bow arm, nock, draw, anchor (target shooting), aim, release, follow-through, and adjusting the sight pin.

TIPS

1. Purchasing a peep sight and stabilizer makes the archery experience more enjoyable and successful.
2. A frequent archery error is dropping the bow arm to see where the arrow is going. This error is called *peeking*. An archer gets in a hurry and peeks to see where the arrow is going, and consequently the arrow drops. Keep the arrow on the string by not peeking. Have patience and wait until the arrow is off the string.
3. If an archer has a problem with inconsistency in accuracy, go to an archery pro shop for suggestions.

EQUIPMENT TIPS

1. There are a variety of bows: strung bows and crossbows, which can be manual or automatic.
2. Carbon graphite arrows, although more expensive than aluminum arrows, are lighter, faster, and stronger.
3. The peep sight is a tiny abettor the archer looks through to align the arrow with the target. The peep sight will force the archer to anchor in the same place for each shot. Anchoring in the same place time after time increases accuracy.
4. The stabilizer assists the archer by quieting the crossbow and placing the pin on target. The stabilizer also prevents the archer from shaking.
5. An archery pro shop is the best place to purchase a bow because the personnel can set the bow up for proper shooting and give specific instruction.
6. The mechanical release is a pull trigger that releases the strings on a crossbow. The trigger provides a quicker, smoother, and more accurate release.
7. Field archers shoot in rough terrain, with three-dimensional targets, from a variety of distances.
8. Bow hunting requires arrows with different points: broad heads for larger game and blunt heads for smaller game. To hunt game birds such as quail, use flu flu arrows.
9. Bow fishing is another unique option.

TEACHING IDEAS

1. Shoot at paper targets with a bull's-eye. Keep score.
2. Shoot to a variety of paper targets. Target shooting during the winter months maintains correct form and technique, thus increasing the archer's ability to hit the game during hunting season.
3. Getting involved in an archery club provides opportunity to learn from the experience of other archers and to improve techniques.
4. To hunt game an archer needs correct equipment, an in-depth knowledge of the ethical principles and laws of hunting game, and correct techniques to harvest the game.

FYI

For further information and special help, consult the following organizations:

National Archery Association
One Olympic Plaza
Colorado Springs, CO 80909
Phone: (719) 578–4576
Fax: (719) 632–4733

The Athletic Institute
200 Castlewood Drive, North
Palm Beach, FL 33408
Phone: 1–800–933–3335

Provides archery videos.

Go to the local pro archery shop for lessons and proper equipment setup.

EQUIPMENT AND SAFETY

Skill	Cue	Common Error
Selecting Bow	Choose a bow that you can draw comfortably and hold for 10 seconds	Bow too heavy
Selecting Arrow	Place nock against chest; reach with fingers; arrow should be 1 inch past fingertips (or draw a marked arrow) Partner stands to the side and reads marking even with bow	Arrow too short or too long
Arm Guard	String should divide the arm guard in half	
Finger Tab or Glove	Protect fingers with tab or glove	String hurts fingers
Safety	Do not draw a bow unless you are on shooting line Do not release a bow without an arrow in it	Bow splits along laminations Injuring students
Retrieving Arrows	Stand to side of arrow; check position of other archers One hand: fingers straddle arrow; press against target Other hand: grasp arrow close to target; rotate and pull straight back	Bending arrow Injuring students

SHOOTING AN ARROW

Skill	Cue	Common Error
Stance Address	Straddle the shooting line (one foot on each side)	Standing behind the line
	Weight even	Leaning forward or backward
	Good posture	
Bow Arm	Grip bow like holding a pop can	Gripping bow too tightly
	Thumb and index finger touch	
	Push bow toward target	
	Elbow points outward	
	Shoulders level	
Nock	Nock arrow at 90-degree angle	Arrow too high or low on string
	Snap nock on bowstring under nock locator	
	Index feather points away from bow	
Draw (Figure 2.1)	Make a scout sign (three fingers up)	More or less than three fingers on string
	String in first groove of index finger	String on fingertips or hand wraps around fingers
	Keep back of hand flat	
	Elbow level with hand	Elbow too low
	Squeeze shoulder blades together	Drawing with arm only
Anchor (Target Shooting) (Figure 2.2)	Touch string to center of chin and center of nose; index finger pushes against jaw bone	Failing to anchor

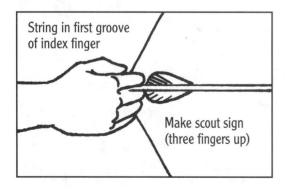

String in first groove of index finger

Make scout sign (three fingers up)

FIGURE 2.1   Draw the Arrow.

SHOOTING AN ARROW

Skill	Cue	Common Error
Aim	Look through pin to center of gold	Looking at target instead of pin
	Aim 3 to 5 seconds prior to releasing	Releasing while drawing
	Close dominant left eye when shooting right-handed	Leaving dominant left eye open when shooting right-handed
Release	Relax fingers	Jerking string hand back or allowing the string to "creep" forward before releasing it
	String "slips" off fingers	
Follow-Through (Hold) (Figure 2.3)	Fingers move back along side of face	Moving string hand
	Hold position until arrow hits target	Moving bow arm
Adjust Sight Pin	Move pin in direction arrows traveled:	Moving sight after each arrow or failing to adjust sight
	If arrows go high, move pin up	
	If arrows go low, move pin down	
	If arrows go left, move pin left	
	If arrows go right, move pin right	

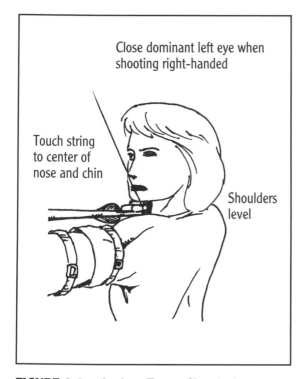

FIGURE 2.2   Anchor (Target Shooting).

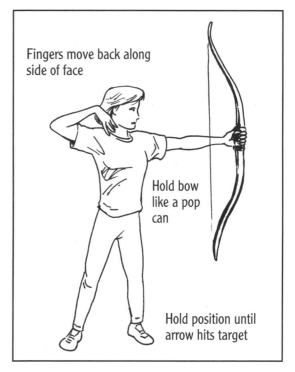

FIGURE 2.3   Follow-Through (Hold).

Chapter 3

Badminton

INTRODUCTION

Badminton is a physically demanding sport that provides players with a good measure of aerobic and anaerobic power, flexibility, strength, and speed. The skills of badminton can be relatively easy to learn, especially with the correct teaching cues. When designing these badminton cues, we consulted the Canadians for their expertise and suggestions. For example, the cue for the wrist action when teaching the badminton overhead clear is "supinate the wrist," which describes clockwise hand rotation; the thumb moves from 9 o'clock to 1 o'clock with palm facing up for a right-handed player. Snapping the wrist would be the common error. This cue and others will provide the teacher with correct teaching techniques.

SKILLS LISTED WITH CUES

A recommended teaching progression of skills before the strokes are taught is as follows: grips, flick up, feeding, ready position, and court position. Teachers should take extra time to teach flick up and feeding skills. The cues for the badminton skills in this chapter include this teaching progression as well as forehand/backhand underhand clear, forehand/backhand overhead clear, forehand/backhand smash, forehand/backhand drive, net shots (finesse shot), long singles serve, short doubles serve, and singles/doubles boundaries, scoring, and strategies.

TIPS

1. Remember . . . correct grip, ready position.
2. Get into the habit of hit-move, hit-move, hit-move.
3. Move to hit the shuttle; don't wait for it.
4. Court sense for singles: after each shot the singles player should attempt to return to base position, which is midcourt. Remember to get in ready position regardless of court position.
5. Court sense for doubles is different. Partners adopt an "up-back" arrangement and, when attacking, a "sides" arrangement. Communicating with and supporting each other is the key to playing a good doubles game.

EQUIPMENT TIPS

1. Shuttles are made of feathers or nylon. One can hit balloons, beach balls, Wiffle balls, or sponge balls.
2. Use tape or cones to mark a court; ropes or lines can be used for the net.
3. Court shoes are recommended.

TEACHING IDEAS

1. Badminton is a demanding game with lots of running, stopping, starting, and lunging. Warm up before stretching. Suggested warm-up activities: light jogging, running in place, jumping jacks, running in various directions, tag games, circuits. After the warm-up, stretch out legs, ankles, arms, and so on.
2. Partner-feed drill: One partner feeds shuttle by hand to the receiver. Receiver hits and then attempts to assume ready position and base position after each return. Cue words are "feed–hit–ready position." Instructor specifies type of hand feed. This drill can be done with or without a net.
3. Racquet-feed drill: same as item 2 but the feeder racquet-feeds to receiver. Feeder gradually sends shuttle to more challenging positions: "further right," "further left," "in front," and "behind" specify the type of feed and type of return.
4. Triples games are designed for large badminton classes. Six can play on a court rather than four. The game is played with three players on each side. Two players from each side are in the front half of the court. Each front player must remain on his or her respective side of the centerline. The third player plays back and may move anywhere in the back half of court. Serve is always from right front position. Team rotates clockwise each time serve is regained.

FYI

For further information and special help, consult the following organizations and sources:

Badminton Canada
1600 James Naismith Drive
Gloucester, Ontario, Canada KIB 5N4
Phone: (613) 748–5605
Fax: (613) 748–5695
Telex: 053 3660

Provides information on instructor manuals, video tapes, drills, skill progressions, program materials, awards, pictures.

U.S. Badminton Association
One Olympic Plaza
Colorado Springs, CO 80909
Phone: (719) 578–4808

Badminton Canada. (1993). *Shuttle*. Ontario, Canada: Badminton Canada.

Reznik, I., & Byrd, R. (1987). *Badminton*. Scottsdale, AZ: Gorsuch Scarisbrick.

BASIC GRIPS AND STANCE

Skill	Cue	Common Error
Forehand Grip	Heel of hand at butt of racquet	Choking up on racquet
	V on top bevel	Grip too tight
	Index finger positioned to pull trigger	Incorrect placement of index finger
	Squeeze trigger finger on impact	
Backhand Grip	Turn racquet clockwise	Failure to rotate grip from forehand to backhand
	Make V on left bevel	
	Knuckle on top	
Ready Position	Elbows on table	
	Knees bent	Standing upright
	Weight on balls of feet	Weight on heels
Forehand Stance	Racquet foot moves toward shuttle	
	Weight shift from back to front like swinging a golf club	Fall backward/fall away

FLICK UP AND FEEDING

Skill	Cue	Common Error
Flick Up		
Definition	Slick move using the racquet to scoop the shuttle from the floor (speeds game up); players must employ proper grip to do this move	
Flick Up Action	Side scooping action, feel snap of wrist as racquet head turns	Forward and up action
	Raise shuttle to land on strings	Improper grip
Feeding		
Definition	Serving the shuttle by hand or by racquet so that receiver has a good chance to return it	

FLICK UP AND FEEDING

Skill	Cue	Common Error
Feeding *(cont.)*		
Hand Position	Hold cork of shuttle with thumb and forefinger	Holding plastic/feathers
	Throw it like a dart to target	Throwing it like a baseball
	Hold shuttle in open hand, cork toward target; throw to target	
	Racquet-high serve and forehand underhand clear are important for feeding (see Serving for cues)	
	Take time to sharpen the feeding skills of players	

CLEARS

Skill	Cue	Common Error
Forehand Underhand Clear	Whip wrist and brush shorts	Snapping wrist
	Contact shuttle below waist	Contacting too soon, lack of height
	Swing up over opposite shoulder	Not following-through, lack of depth
Forehand Overhead Clear	Supinate hand; thumb rotates from 9 to 1 o'clock, clockwise for a right-handed player; palm rolls up (Figure 3.1)	Snapping wrist
		Not extending elbow

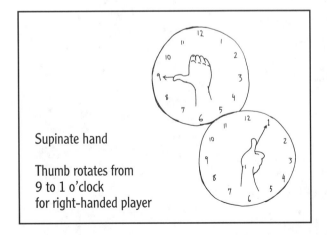

Supinate hand

Thumb rotates from
9 to 1 o'clock
for right-handed player

FIGURE 3.1   Hand Action for Forehand Overhead Clear.

Reach up; contact shuttle high in front of body

Push from back to forward foot

FIGURE 3.2 Forehand Overhead Clear.

CLEARS		
Skill	**Cue**	**Common Error**
Forehand Overhead Clear *(cont.)*	Supinate hand; thumb rotates from 3 to 11 o'clock, counterclockwise for a left-handed player; palm rolls up	Snapping wrist
	Reach up and contact shuttle high in front of body, like throwing something on roof	
	Whip!	
	Push from back to forward foot (Figure 3.2)	Weight forward

SMASH—DRIVES—NET SHOTS		
Skill	**Cue**	**Common Error**
Forehand Smash	Lean into the net	
	Contact shuttle in front of body	Contacting shuttle behind head
	Supinate hand; thumb rotates from 9 to 1 o'clock, clockwise for a right-handed player; palm moves up	Snapping wrists

SMASH—DRIVES—NET SHOTS

Skill	Cue	Common Error
Forehand Smash (cont.)	Supinate hand; thumb rotates from 3 to 11 o'clock, counterclockwise for a left-handed player; palm moves up	
	Wrist starts cocked, finishes in supinated position	
	Whip action	
	Swing is half moon with faced racquet pointing down at contact	Swinging too long or too short
Forehand Drive	Move racquet foot toward shuttle	Feet are stationary
	Contact more to the side of body, like throwing a ball sidearm	Contact too high or too low
	Punch/whip/crack	
Backhand Drive	Same as forehand; change grip	
Net Shot (Finesse Shot) (Figure 3.3)	Loosen grip	Firm grip
	Be gentle; slide racquet under shuttle	Swinging at shuttle
	Focus on palm of hand; lift shuttle over, use arm only, not racquet	Hitting hard
	Push/lift/nudge/caress	

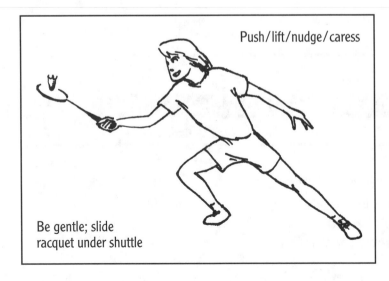

Push/lift/nudge/caress

Be gentle; slide racquet under shuttle

FIGURE 3.3 Net Shot (Finesse Shot).

SERVING		
Skill	**Cue**	**Common Error**
Long Singles Service	Bend knees and swing under and up	Side swing
	Contact out in front of body	Contact behind body
	Swing under shuttle	
	Follow-through straight up to hit face with biceps	No follow-through
Short Doubles Service	Drop the shuttle before you swing	Throwing shuttle up
	Shorten back swing	Long back swing
	Keep wrist firm	Snapping wrist
	Watch contact	Eyes lose sight of shuttle
	Push through the shuttle	Hitting shuttle
Boundaries (Figure 3.4)		
Singles	Tall skinny man	
Doubles	Short fat man	

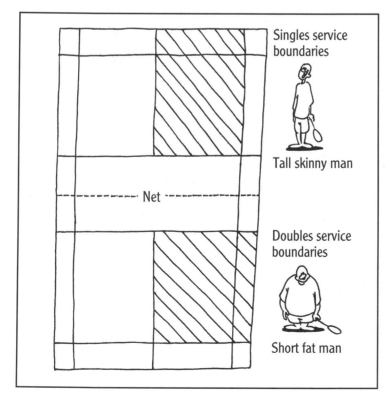

FIGURE 3.4 Service Boundaries for Singles and Doubles.

SINGLES RULES—SCORING—STRATEGIES

Skill	Cue	Common Error
Scoring	Only the server can score points	
	1 point scored when opposing player fails to return shuttle back over net	
	1 point scored when shuttle comes back over the net and lands out of bounds	
	Server serves in right court when server's score is 0 or even	
	Server serves in left court when server's score is odd	
Boundaries	Tall skinny man	
Men's Singles	Played to 15 points	Forgetting to take the option to set when score is tied
Setting	13–13 set 5	
	14–14 set 3	
	First player to 13 has option to set to 5; start game over and play to 5 points	Starting score at 13 and playing to 17
	First player to 14 has option to set to 3; start game over and play to 3 points	Starting score at 14 and playing to 17
Match Play	Player who wins two out of three games wins the match	
Women's Singles	Played to 11 points	
Setting	9–9, set 3	Forgetting to take the option to set when score is tied
	10–10, set 2	
	First player to reach 9 has option to set to 3; start game over and play to 3 points	Starting score at 9 and playing to 12
	First player to reach 10 has option to set to 2; start game over and play to 2 points	Starting score at 10 and playing to 12
Match Play	Player who wins two out of three games wins the match	
Strategies	Play opponent's weak side	Playing opponent's forehand side
	Mix up shots; be unpredictable	Using same shot

SINGLES RULES—SCORING—STRATEGIES

Skill	Cue	Common Error
Strategies *(cont.)*	Use deception, and disguise shots	
	Use clears to force opponent deep in court and on the move	Hitting shuttle to middle of court
	Mix shots and make your opponent run to weaken his return; then take advantage of the weak return with a well-placed powerful smash	
	The patient aggressive player wins points	

DOUBLES RULES—SCORING—STRATEGIES

Skill	Cue	Common Error
Front/Back (Figure 3.5)	"Up/back formation" in attack mode after a smash or drop	
	Front player—halfway between service line and net	
	Back player—shadow to front player	
Side to Side (Figure 3.6)	When defending or in trouble, use side position that is parallel to partner	

Front player halfway between service line and net

Shadow to front player

FIGURE 3.5 Doubles Formation for Attack Mode after a Smash or Drop.

Use side position that is parallel to partner

Each player covers own property line

FIGURE 3.6 Doubles Formation When Defending or in Trouble.

DOUBLES RULES—SCORING—STRATEGIES

Skill	Cue	Common Error
Side to Side (cont.)	Each player covers own property line	
	Stay within property line	Crossing over line
Basic Guidelines	Support partner in every way possible	
	Always be ready to cover for partner	
	Don't get in each other's way; let partner take his or her own shots	
	Call for "iffy" (in-between) shots ("mine")	
	Whenever possible send shots between opponents so as to confuse them	
Inning	A doubles team has an "inning," meaning both players are entitled to serve	
Starting Position	Start in right-hand court	
	One hand in first inning (one server)	
	Two hands in each inning after (two servers)	
Server	Server alternates serving court each time point is made	
Receivers	Receivers do not change courts	
Scoring	Serve to score	
Points	15-point games; must win by 2 points	
Match	Win two out of three games	
Break	5-minute rest period between game 2 and 3	

Chapter 4

Baseball

INTRODUCTION

"There is no joy in Mudville: mighty Casey has struck out." What the fans in joyless Mudville never knew about their mighty slugger Casey is that after striking out, Casey decided to ask his coach how to improve his batting skills. Casey's coaches now face the challenge of correcting Casey's swing and restoring joy to Mudville.

Selecting critical errors and giving the right cue is not an easy task for the coach. The cues in this chapter were designed to help the coaches analyze skill and provide effective cues. For example, the cue "Imagine the middle of baseball has a face on it and the face is laughing at you; try to hit the ball in the face" helps the batter focus on the ball and improve batting technique.

SKILLS LISTED WITH CUES

This chapter presents cues for the following baseball skills: hitting, throwing, fielding ground balls and fly balls, bunting, pitching (fastball, curveball, slider, knuckleball, forkball, screwball), catching, and sliding (feet first, head first).

TIPS

1. Warm up with a fungo bat. This drill teaches quick hands, increasing bat speed. Warming up with heavy bats teaches your hands to drag the bat through the strike zone.
2. Run a couple of laps around the bases or park before stretching out and warming up the arm. This activity warms the arm up a little faster and helps circulate the blood.
3. Start with short-distance throwing and move into a long toss. A long toss is defined as throwing the ball as far as one can but still keeping it on the line. The long toss is the only true way to increase arm strength, and it also feels good.
4. Use the fungo bat for batting-tee drills, soft-toss drills, and warming up before hitting. Bat speed is the goal.

EQUIPMENT TIPS

1. Gloves: infielders need short-pocket gloves, and outfielders need large-pocket gloves.
2. Bats: pick a bat that is comfortable in the hands, one that is not too heavy or long. The key in hitting is bat speed.
3. A fungo bat is used to hit infield balls. These bats are not made for hitting pitched balls. The bat will break hitting a pitched ball.
4. Baseball metal spikes on shoes are preferred because they help with traction.
5. Batting gloves protect the hands when hitting, and they also provide protection under the mitt. They also provide protection when base running. The runner should hold the batting gloves in clenched fists to protect fingers when sliding.
6. Wiffle balls can be used for soft-toss drills. They can also be used for batting practice in a very small area if a cage is not available. A player can use Wiffle balls for batting practice before games. The use of Wiffle balls avoids damage to fences. Baseballs have a tendency to bend a chain-link fence (Figure 4.1).
7. Catcher equipment is needed for protection: shin guards, chest protector, helmet, cup, mask, and throat guard.
8. Baseball caps are critical to help block the sun.

TEACHING IDEAS

1. *Batting Drill Stations:* To develop the necessary techniques and rhythm to hit a live pitch, many repetitions of a correct swing are necessary. The emphasis in these drills should be on trigger position, hand action, and hip rotation.
   a. *Soft-Toss Drill:* The batter hits into a fence or net. Another player kneels facing the batter, a short distance off the batter's front foot, and tosses underhand. As he lowers his hand to toss, the batter cocks the bat as he would when a pitcher delivers a ball.

Soft-toss drill using Wiffle balls

Fence undamaged

Use Wiffle balls

FIGURE 4.1 Wiffle Balls Used for Soft-Toss Drills.

b. *Batting Tee:* A tee is used, and the ball is rotated to different positions to give the batter a variety of areas to hit.

c. *Hip Drill:* Use a plastic bat. Coach gets behind batter, places hands on hips, and helps turn or snap batter's hips.

d. *Pitching:* The pitcher pitches the ball to the hitter, or a pitching machine is used.

2. *Two-Tee Drill:* Set one batting tee in the inside corner. The player will hit the ball down the left-field line. Set another batting tee on the outside batting corner, player will hit the ball down the right-field line. Instructor stands behind the tees. After the batter cocks front shoulder and starts forward, instructor yells "inside" or "outside"; then batter hits said tee.

3. *Four-Corners Drill:* Four to 12 players on the four bases throw the ball around the bases. The goal is to try to catch the ball in the catching zone. (The catching zone is the top left-hand side toward the glove side, to the left of the heart for a right-handed player.) This drill teaches players to shuffle feet and have a quick ball exchange. Modifications of four-corners drill: catch, shuffle, throw; hop, chase.

FYI

For further information and special help, consult the following organization:

Rocky Mountain School of Baseball
560 West 600 North
Logan, UT 84321
Phone: (801) 753–5662

Provides information on camps and tournaments, as well as fundamentals, college evaluations, and video critiques.

BATTING

Skill	Cue	Common Error
Hitting		
Stance	Stand sideways	Stand forward
	Feet slightly wider than shoulder width	Feet too far apart or too close together
	Weight over balls of feet, heels lightly touching the ground, more weight on back leg	Weight on heels
Arm Swing	Hitter should think "shoulder to shoulder" (start with chin on front shoulder; finish swing with chin on back shoulder)	Moving head during the swing Head too tense
Hip Rotation	Back hip snaps or rotates at pitcher; drive body through ball; take photograph of pitcher with belly button	No hip rotation
	Throw hands through baseball: "slow feet, quick hands"	Using arms instead of wrists
Focus of Eyes	Imagine middle of baseball has a face that is laughing at you; try to hit the ball in the face (Figure 4.2)	Not seeing ball hit bat
	Watch ball all the way into catcher's mitt	
Step	Step 3 to 6 inches (stride should be more of a glide)	Overstriding causes bat to drop during swing (jarring step)
	"Step to hit"	Hitter "steps and then hits"
Follow-Through	Top hand rolls over bottom hand; bat goes all around the body	
Recommended Progression	Teach cues in order listed; when first three are mastered, add others	
Bunting	Pivot toward pitcher; square body to pitcher	Hitter or bunter does not get properly squared around in position to bunt
	Slide top hand up bat; keep bat level at all times. Keep fingers behind bat or protect fingers from ball	Hands remain together (bat is not kept level if pitch is either high or low); wrap hand around bat
	Catch ball with bat	Push bat at ball, swipe at ball

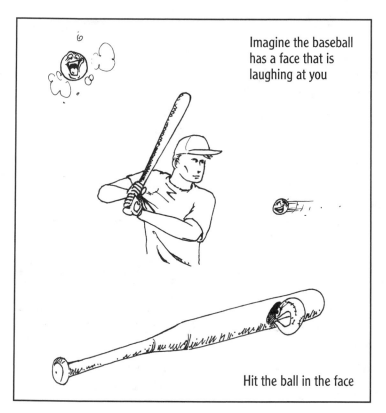

Imagine the baseball has a face that is laughing at you

Hit the ball in the face

FIGURE 4.2 Focus of Eyes When Hitting a Baseball.

HITTING—INEXPERIENCED BATTERS		
Skill	**Cue**	**Common Error**
Checkpoints for Coaches	If the batter is not gripping, standing, or holding bat correctly, coach could correct the player individually	Don't use these cues unless a player needs assistance; give one at a time
Grip	Hold bat in base of fingers (this technique allows wrist to roll freely and generates bat speed) Align knuckles	Bat held in palm of hand, squeezing bat
Closed Stance	Feet are shoulder-width apart; then front foot is placed toward plate (helps untrained hitter step toward pitcher)	Stepping back

HITTING—INEXPERIENCED BATTERS

Skill	Cue	Common Error
Bat Position	Bat held armpit high and far enough away from the body that two players' fists could fit	Bat held too close to shoulder
	Back elbow held away from body	Back elbow drops
Bat Angle	Straight up in air or up and angled slightly over back shoulder	Cradling bat around head; bat is pointing back toward pitcher

THROWING

Skill	Cue	Common Error
Grip	Get a seam, either across the seams or with the seams	Not getting a seam, poor control of ball
	Hold ball with fingertips: first two fingers on top of ball, second two underneath to the side, thumb opposite side	Holding baseball in palm or placing more fingers on top of ball
Stance	Stand sideways, ankle eye toward target	Standing facing the target
Throwing Action	Point glove-hand shoulder at target	Staying square to target (no shoulder or hip rotation is possible)
	Take a long step toward target	Stepping across body, no step at all, or a step that is too high
	Stretch arm way back	
	Make L shape with throwing arm	Taking the ball directly behind head with bent elbow
	Pull glove arm down, and replace glove arm with throwing arm	
	Whip the arm through, snap wrist	No wrist action, all arm
	Follow-through, wrist goes to opposite knee—slap knee	No follow-through

FIELDING—GROUND BALLS

Skill	Cue	Common Error
Stance	Feet shoulder-width apart, weight on balls of feet (right-handers lead slightly with left foot because the slight lead of the left foot means that less time is needed to rotate body to throw)	Weight on heels, feet too close or too far apart
	Create a triangle with both feet and glove; the glove is the apex (top) of the triangle	Glove inside or behind knees
	Bend at knees; slightly at waist	Bending at waist and not knees
Catching Action	Field ball out in front	Trying to play ball behind the legs
	Keep glove close to or on ground	Starting with glove waist high and trying to go down at ball
	Elbows inside knees	Knees inside of elbows, loose coordination
	Put your nose on the ball; follow the ball into glove with eyes	Pulling head up; not seeing ball into glove in fear of being hit in the face
	Secure ball with both hands	Fielding ball with only the glove
	Read a hop; read the path of baseball; try to field ball on big or long hop; after a big hop ball will usually stay low	Letting ball dictate way to play it (letting ball play fielder)

FIELDING—FLY BALLS

Skill	Cue	Common Error
Stance	Comfortable stance, weight on balls of feet	Rigid, fight stance; weight on back of heels like a boxer
Catching Position	Position body underneath flight of baseball (the path should becoming down to the eyes)	Having to catch ball behind your head or below your waist
Catching Action	Place glove slightly out from and above head; reach for the sky with fingers just before the ball arrives	Catching ball to side of body; fingers stretched out rather than up
	Always use two hands to secure ball	One-handed "showboat"
	Follow ball into glove with eyes	Not watching ball all the way into glove

PITCHING

Skill	Cue	Common Error
Delivery	Step directly toward home plate	Foot goes too far one way or the other
	Use normal throwing motion, nice and easy "loosey goosey"	Overthrowing, trying to throw the ball too hard; avoid sidearming
	Use legs to generate power, push with back leg	Relying too much on arm
	Simply play catch with catcher, throw strikes	Trying to do too much, overthrowing and not throwing any strikes
	Comfortable, smooth delivery	No rhythm
Pitches		
Fastball	Grip with seams for a sink action; grip across seam for a rise	Wrong grip or simply grabbing ball
	Pressure on fingertips	No pressure points
	Smooth delivery	Rushed motion
	Wrist snap	No wrist action

PITCHING		
Skill	**Cue**	**Common Error**
Pitches (*cont.*)		
Curveball	Grip with seams	Wrong grip
	Fastball motion	Motion too slow and obvious
	Reduce speed of ball	Too much speed, no rotation or spin
	Tickle ear	Not cocking wrist
	Pull down	Lazy arm action
	Snap fingers	Letting ball simply roll off fingers
Slider	Backward C	Wrong grip and placement of fingers
	Off center	Holding ball in center
	Fastball speed and motion	Slow or rushed motion
	Turn wrist over or turn doorknob	Throwing like a curveball, cocking wrist
	Second finger	First finger releases ball
Knuckleball	Fingernail grip	Knuckles on seams
	Dig seams	Not enough pressure on seams
	Extend and push toward plate	Forcing the ball
	Stiff wrist	Snapping the wrist
Forkball	Make fork shape with fingers	Fingers not far enough apart
	Fingers outside seams	Fingers directly on seams
	Ball rolls away	Pressure on fingertips
	No wrist action or snap	Too much wrist
Screwball	Grip narrow seams	Simply grabbing baseball
	Overhand	Sidearm
	Inside out	Curveball motion
	Reverse snap	Not enough wrist action
	Thumb flip	No thumb

CATCHING

Skill	Cue	Common Error
Catcher's Stance (Figure 4.3)	Feet outside shoulders	Kneeling
	Head up	Head down
	Chest on knees	
	Place throwing arm behind back	Placing arm directly behind or to the side of the catcher's mitt is more likely to cause injury
	Catch the ball using both hands	Relying solely on catcher's mitt
	Use body as wall to block pitches	
	Move to ball	Reaching for ball

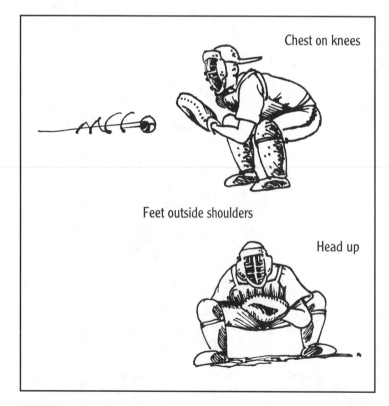

FIGURE 4.3 Catcher's Stance.

SLIDING

Skill	Cue	Common Error
Feet First	Sprint	Slowing up
	Slide early	Sliding too late (injuries)
	Sit down	Falling and hopping
	Curl leg under, making a figure 4	Sliding with both legs forward
	Roller-coaster ride	Lying down completely
Head First	Sprint	Slowing down
	Sink	Upright and no balance
	Dive	Belly flopping into base
	Outstretched arms	Hands and arms too close to body
	Superman in flight	

Chapter 5

Basketball

INTRODUCTION

Larry Bird, one of the best triple-threat players of all time, presented a great danger to his defenders because of three options he could take from the triple-threat position: passing, shooting, and dribbling.

The game of basketball requires a variety of skills, but all of these skills have things in common. Commonalities reduce the stimuli students and players need to take in and simplify the processing of information. The more interrelated the skills appear to be, the more quickly they are internalized. For example, the concept of triple threat represents the beginning place for shooting, passing, and dribbling. These skills should be taught as variations of the same theme rather than as separate, unrelated skills.

An integral and accepted strategy for teaching motor skills is the use of cues. Current teaching strategies, such as the knowledge-structure (KS) approach presented by Vickers (1990), emphasize cues as a fundamental component. Cues are referred to as "keys to success" in the KS method.

Cues may be verbal in nature, and they may serve as short reminders of more complete information presented about a skill. A verbal cue for shooting-hand preparation in a set shot is "palm up." Phrases may also be more visual in nature with the intent of creating a picture in the learner's mind that results in correct skill performance. The palm-up cue could be followed by "holding a waiter's tray."

SKILLS LISTED WITH CUES

This chapter presents teaching cues for the following basketball skills: set shot, jump shot, free throw, right- and left-handed layups, dribbling, basic ball-handling position, passing, blocking out, rebounding, defensive stance, going for a ball out of bounds, and pivoting. These cues can generally be used at all levels of instruction.

TIPS

1. Because players need to be able to control the ball while moving in different directions, teach them to dribble with both the right and left hand.
2. Begin dribbling drills with emphasis on looking up. Play heads-up ball.

EQUIPMENT TIPS

1. Providing coed students (upper middle school through college) with both men's and women's regulation size balls allows them to choose the ball that feels most comfortable.

   - Coed: provide both balls.
   - Women's teams: provide a women's size basketball.
   - Men's teams: provide a men's regulation ball.

2. Scoreboards: plastic flip scoreboards and electric scoreboards.
3. Coed games: shorten three-point line for girls; boys, one point inside key, two points outside key, three points outside three-point line.
4. Provide each team with a different color pinnie for their uniforms.
5. Use poster board to display team scores for tournament. Teams like to know their standings in the tournament.

TEACHING IDEAS

1. Random dribbling around a gymnasium, dribbling under control, keeping head up and anticipating the space one will need. Teach various methods of dribble crossover, pivot, and crossover reverse pivot. Goal is to keep head up, manipulate the ball in a confusing space, develop ball control, and learn space orientation and head-ups dribbling.
2. Play half-court games with large classes.
3. The clock and the electric scoreboard are used by the two teams who have won "king of the court." Players love to see the numbers flash on a scoreboard.
4. Keep daily point total for each team's score, for all teams in a weeklong tournament. The team with the most points for the entire tournament wins. Ideas for rewarding the winning teams—first-place players win movie tickets; second-place, soda pop; and third-place, bubblegum.
5. Play two cross-court games, six players per team. Four players play in game, the player who scores sits out, and a sideline player replaces the player who just scored. This game gives everybody an opportunity to score, and every player is rotated in. Two games are being played at the same time. Students who do not dress out or those who are injured or sick keep score and referee. Referee's decision is final.
6. End class sessions by holding short competitions. For example, everybody takes a turn to shoot a half-court shot, free throw competition, dribble tag competition.

FYI

For further information and special help, consult the following organizations:

National Basketball Association
645 Fifth Avenue
New York, NY 10022
Phone: (212) 407–8000

USA Basketball
One Olympic Plaza
Colorado Springs, CO 80909

SET SHOT

Skill	Cue	Common Error
Set-Up (Figure 5.1)		
Shooting Hand	Spread fingers	
	Palm up; balance a waiter's tray	Ball held in palm
Nonshooting Hand	Hand faces side wall; fingers only touch ball	
Alignment	Arm, eye, and hand lined up with basket, like throwing a dart	Push ball sideways
		Arm at 45-degree angle
		Elbow points to side
Sight	Focus on back edge of rim	
	Basket looks like a big bin	
Legs	Slightly bend knees and buttocks out	Insufficient force from no use of legs
Balance	Body square to basket	
Shooting Action		
Fingers	Spin ball off middle and index finger: fast spin, lines on ball not visible	Ball is thrown
Wrist	Flip wrist, wave good-bye to ball	Inadequate wrist action

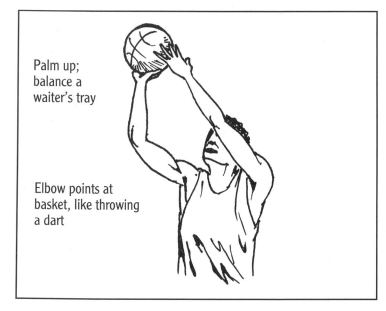

Palm up; balance a waiter's tray

Elbow points at basket, like throwing a dart

FIGURE 5.1   Set Shot—Set-Up.

SET SHOT

Skill	Cue	Common Error
Shooting Action *(cont.)*		
Shoot Over	Shoot up over a telephone booth	Insufficient drive upward, loss of balance
Path of Ball	Make a rainbow; put it in the pot of gold	
Finish Position (Figure 5.2)		
Wrist	Gooseneck finish, thumb points at shoes	Lack of follow-through
	Everything stays in a straight line	
	Wrist points at rim or put finger in basket	
	Follow shot	Fall backward or relax

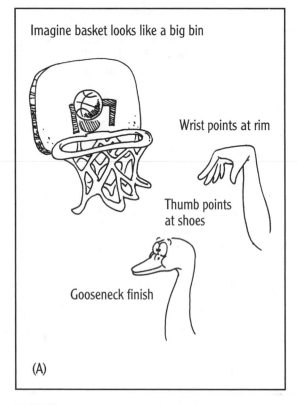

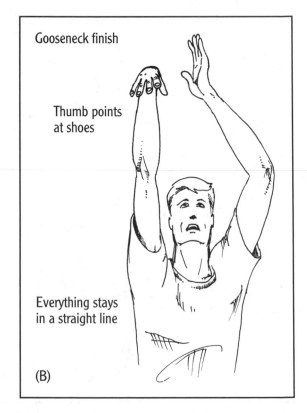

FIGURE 5.2 Set Shot—Finish Position (A) Side view, (B) Front view.

JUMP SHOT

Skill	Cue	Common Error
Arm and Hand Preparation	Bring back of hand to forehead in preparation, as if holding a waiter's tray over head	Hand is off line, insufficient force from wrist
Shooting Action	Same as the set shot	Shooting from behind head
Timing	Jump—hang—then shoot Shot released at top of jump	Shooting on way up

FREE THROW

Skill	Cue	Common Error
Set Shot	Refer to Set Shot cues (pp 43–44) with a couple of exceptions	
Set-Up, Feet Parallel	Feet square Both toes on foul line, shoulder width apart	Line violation
Offset Stance	One foot slightly forward	Line violation
Ritual	Prepare	No routine, no high-percentage shots
	Breathe/relax	
	Focus/visualize	
	Shoot	Rushing shot; distracted—not concentrating
	Mental imagery at different times during the day	

LAY-UPS		
Skill	**Cue**	**Common Error**
Right-Handed		
Steps	Step right, left, hop (jump)	Jumping off wrong foot
	Right knee up (90 degrees)	
	Reach: shoot at peak of hop and reach	Shooting ball more likely to be blocked
Shooting Hand	Underhand, laying up ball softly as if the ball is an egg	Not softening shot enough
	Extend arm, reach high (ball kisses backboard)	Hitting backboard too hard or soft
	Release at peak of reach	
	Soften shot because of speed	Not compensating for speed
Shot Focus	Square on backboard	Looking at dribble, not focused on aim
Left-Handed		
Steps	Step left, right, hop (jump)	Jumping off wrong foot
	Left knee up (90 degrees)	
Shooting Action	Left hand shoots ball	Using wrong hand on wrong side

DRIBBLING		
Skill	**Cue**	**Common Error**
Position of Hands (Figure 5.3)	Fingers spread, stretch fingers	Fingers together
	Wrist firm but movable	Lack of tension in the wrist
	Pads of fingers control ball	Palm touches ball
Forearm and Wrist Action	Action from forearm, pushing action	Slapping ball with wrist action
	Absorb ball back into pads of fingers (hesitation in hand): "spring action"	Slapping ball, not absorbing the ball
	Ball attached to hand, you and ball are one: "yo-yo action"	Treating ball as obstacle apart from self

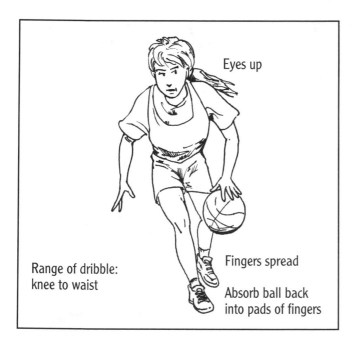

Eyes up

Range of dribble:
knee to waist

Fingers spread

Absorb ball back
into pads of fingers

FIGURE 5.3   Dribbling Action.

DRIBBLING		
Skill	**Cue**	**Common Error**
Hand Placement— More Complex Dribble	Move hand on different angles of ball	Palming the ball (carrying the ball)
Eyes	"Keep eyes *up*"	Do not watch ball
Height of Dribble	Below waist	Dribble too high
Range of Dribble	Knee to waist	Dribble to hear yourself dribble
Overall Rules— More Complex Dribble	Higher dribble for higher speed Lower dribble for lower speeds and tight situations	Not advancing the ball Dribble without purpose
Body Protection	Protect ball with body but see basket Protect/shields ball if guarded	Turning back to teammates and basket

BASIC BALL-HANDLING

Skill	Cue	Common Error
Ready Position (Figure 5.4)	"Triple threat" Purpose: to fake out opponent with the option of the following skills: shooting, passing, dribbling	Not assuming the position
Hand Position	Shooting position on ball	Hands not in shooting position; hands too close together
Holding Ball	Hold ball to side on hip Keep ball on hip—hold ball to side to pass, dribble, or step into shot Elbows out	Ball held too high or too low

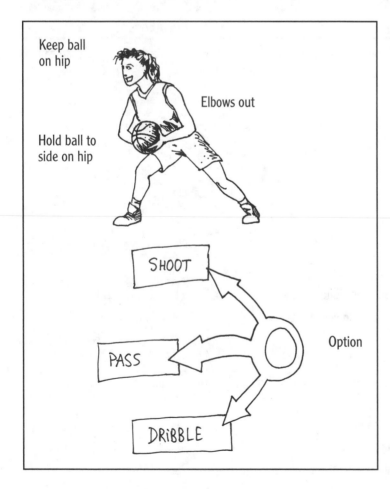

FIGURE 5.4 Basic Ball-Handling Position—"Triple Threat."

PASSING

Skill	Cue	Common Error
Two-Hand Chest Pass		
Hand Position	Hand on side of ball, thumbs pointing to each other	Dominant hand does most of the pushing
Throwing Action	Step forward with preferred foot	No forward step or transfer of weight
Elbows	Push ball forward from chest, elbows out; snap it	
Finish Position	Thumbs down	
	Backs of hands facing each other	
	Transfer weight to front foot	
Two-Hand Overhead Pass		
Arm Action	Ball overhead, like a soccer throw-in	Misuse of pass
	Strong wrist flip	Not using both hands equally

BLOCKING OUT

Skill	Cue	Common Error
Action of Body	Find with hands	
Turn Back to Opponent (Figure 5.5)	Put buttocks under opponent's hip or create a stable wall between opponent and ball	Not able to hold position
Hands (after Pivot)	Elbows out, palms wide; feel for opponent	

Create a stable wall between opponent and ball

Elbows out— palms wide, feel for opponent

Put buttocks under opponent's hip

FIGURE 5.5 Blocking Out.

REBOUNDING		
Skill	**Cue**	**Common Error**
Timing	Hesitate	Jumping too soon or late
	Catch ball at height of jump	
Hands/Arms	Grab ball with both hands	Trying to tip the ball with one hand and possibly to someone else
	Strong hands, elbows out, fingers spread	Elbowing in, fingers together
Go to Ball	Jump to ball	
Body Position for Defensive Rebounding	Buttocks out, elbows out, ball in	Exposing ball to opponents in traffic
	Protect ball with body	
	Outlet pass or dribble out	Ball stolen or tied up as rebounder stands and looks
Body Position for Offensive Rebounding	Protect the ball	Exposing ball to traffic
	Tip ball to basket or assume shooting position as quickly as possible, like a "pogo stick"	Bringing ball down and getting set or dribbling

DEFENSIVE STANCE		
Skill	**Cue**	**Common Error**
Stance (Figure 5.6)	Weight on balls of feet	
	Wide stance	Stance too wide
	Knees bent, body low, like a sumo wrestler	Surfer's stance, legs straight
Leg and Foot Action	Shuffle step, do not cross feet	Weight back
	Knees bent	Straight leg shuffle
	Heel-to-toe foot placement	Bouncing on toes
Offense Dribbles	Palms up, swat up	Hands not moving
	One hand up, one hand down, hands active	
Offense Prepares to Shoot or Pass	Like putting handprints on a mirror	Resting hands and arms on defense
	Cut off passing lane	
Rules Off Ball	See both: see ball, see opponent	Playing too far from ball
		Losing sight of ball

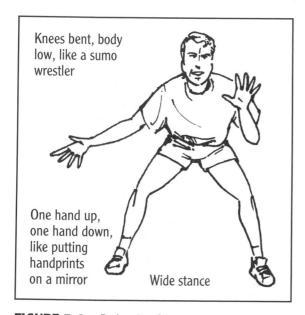

Knees bent, body low, like a sumo wrestler

One hand up, one hand down, like putting handprints on a mirror

Wide stance

FIGURE 5.6   Defensive Stance.

PIVOTING		
Skill	**Cue**	**Common Error**
Stance (Figure 5.7)	Toes of pivot foot pinned or nailed to floor	Dragging pivot foot
Movement	Anchored to floor Stepping all directions, forward and backward	Traveling
Going for a Ball out of Bounds (Figure 5.8)	Sacrifice your body Grasp the ball Dive to the ground	Watching a perfectly fair ball go out of bounds

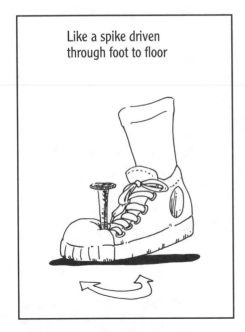

Like a spike driven through foot to floor

FIGURE 5.7 Pivoting.

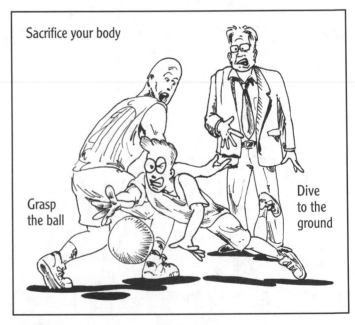

Sacrifice your body

Grasp the ball

Dive to the ground

FIGURE 5.8 Going for a Ball out of Bounds.

Chapter 6

Bowling

INTRODUCTION

"Strike!" The crashing of the pins fills the air with excitement and anticipation of bowling the perfect game of 300. Families, friends, coworkers, and peers can all join in the fun of bowling. How does one learn to bowl? Many bowlers learn by trial and error. Teachers offering bowling in their curriculum could use the cues in this chapter to explain the skills of bowling, even when a bowling alley is not available. (How do you add bowling but not a bowling alley to your curriculum? See equipment tips.)

SKILLS LISTED WITH CUES

Teachers can use simple instructional cues in this chapter to teach the following bowling skills: grip, stance, arm action and leg action on approach and delivery, delivering a straight ball and hook ball, use of arrows for spares and placement of feet, and finding an eye target for spares, splits, and adjustments. Because scoring the game of bowling can be confusing and frustrating to the beginning bowler, we have added scoring cues.

We hope that these cues will help students be more comfortable with bowling and that they will seek real bowling opportunities. Friends can go bowling and experience success together.

TIPS

1. Remain behind the foul line at all times.
2. Never walk in front of another bowler.
3. Give the bowler to your right the right-of-way.
4. Remain quiet while other students are bowling.

EQUIPMENT TIPS

1. Gym floor.
2. Rubber bowling balls can be ordered, or round soccer nerf balls can be used.
3. Pins can be made from two-liter pop bottles or empty tennis ball cans, or white plastic pins can be ordered.

4. Scorecards can be obtained from a local bowling alley.
5. Long ropes can be used for lane dividers, or a gym wall can be one side of a lane.
6. Use colored tape for lane arrows and *x*'s to mark the spots where the pins stand.

TEACHING IDEAS

1. Have students practice technique and scoring in gym. Have two lines back to back at center court. Pair up in partners (bowl to wall, take turns with balls).
2. Same drill as above except bowl to one pin only, progress to three pins, five pins, and all 10 pins. Work on technique. Scoring options: Set one pin up; if they knock one pin down, award one point. Set three pins up; if they knock three pins down, score one point. Set five pins up; knock five pins down to score one point. Team competition: Four on a team; set three pins up; count number of pins knocked down by team, have a five-minute time limit. One student bowls; the other runs the ball down to partner; and the other two set up pins. Rotate after they finish their frame at bowling (Figure 6.1). Work on fitness and bowling skills.

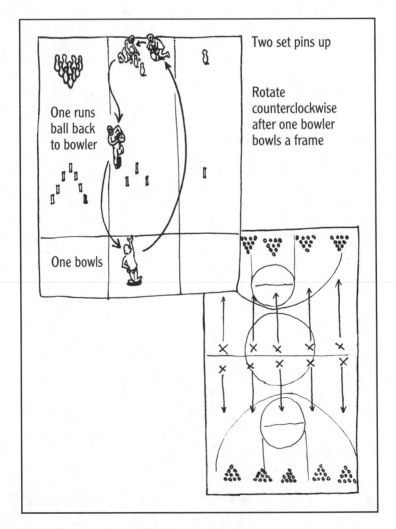

FIGURE 6.1 Game-like Fitness Drill.

3. Teach scoring with 10 pins in gym. Get bowling cards from local bowling alleys. Even teams of four. One student bowls, one student runs the ball down to bowler, one sets up pins, one keeps score; rotate after these finish their frame at bowling. These drills and scoring system add fitness to the lesson, and the students enjoy the competition.

4. Handicapping is used in bowling to create parity between bowlers and stimulate greater competition. The following rules and formulas are used when computing a handicap.

   a. A minimum of nine games must be bowled before students can compute a handicap

   b. Handicap = (200 − Average score) × 0.8

   c. Average score = total points ÷ number of games

   d. The handicap is added to each player's total score at the end of a game during tournament play, as in the following example:

Joe bowls the following scores for nine games: 107, 113, 121, 115, 135, 101, 112, 115, 140
(107 + 113 + 121 +115 + 135 + 101 + 112 + 115 + 140) ÷ 9 = 117.6
Joe's average number of pins per game is 117.6. To compute his handicap
(200 − 117.6) × 0.8 = 65.87
Joe bowls Frank in the tournament. Joe gets a final score of 132, and Frank's score is 159.
Joe's handicap is 66, and Frank's handicap is 63. The final scores are as follows:
Joe—132 + 66 = 198   Frank—159 + 63 = 222   Frank wins the tournament.

FYI

For further information and special help, consult the following organizations and source:

American Bowling Congress (ABC) coordinator at local bowling center.

Young American Bowling Alliance (YABA)
5301 South 76th Street
Green Dale, WI 53129–1127
Phone: (414) 423–3421
Fax: (414) 421–1194

Ask about the In-School Bowling Program (a great teaching tool). They will send out a complete learning package on bowling. Included in this package are pamphlets, bowling etiquette, scoring information, skills, instructional video, coloring books on scoring.

Harrison, M., & Maxey, R. (1987). *Bowling*. Glenview, IL: Scott, Foresman.

BASIC GRIPS AND STANCE

Skill	Cue	Alternate Cue	Common Error
Grip			
Conventional	Thumb on top, handshake position	Thumb hole at 12:00, finger holes at 6:00	
	Grip ball with second groove of two middle fingers	Ring finger and middle finger	Squeezing with thumb
Fingertip	Cradle ball in opposite arm		
	Grip ball with first groove of two middle fingers		Thumb in first Squeezing with thumb
Stance	Erect, knees relaxed	Stand tall	Knees locked, shoulders not square to pins
	Ball supported by non-delivery arm	Ball carried on palm of right hand	Ball hanging from thumb and fingers
	Ball on right side	Ball hides right shirt pocket (good place to start); find your comfort zone	Ball too high or low
	Lower right shoulder	Tilt body slightly to right	
	Feet slightly apart	Three boards between feet	
	Left foot slightly advanced (Figure 6.2)	One-half foot length ahead	
	Eyes focus on aiming spot	Look at second arrow from right	Looking at pins

APPROACH			
Skill	**Cue**	**Alternate Cue**	**Common Error**
Arm Action (Figure 6.3)	First step and arm push away together	Step away, push away	Stepping before pushing away
	Extend ball arm straight forward horizontally	Long reach but short step, like handing ball to friend	Pushing ball up or to the right too far
	Use pendulum swing, like ball on end of string	Ball falls downward and backward	Applying too much force changing direction of ball
	Ball swings back, shoulder high	Horizontal in front to horizontal in back	Ball goes too high or arcs behind body
	Extend left arm outward for balance		
	Keep ball swinging, arms relaxed	Gravity and inertia provide main force	Trying to throw ball too fast
	Release ball as arm passes vertical	Ball should land 3 to 4 feet beyond foul line	Dropping ball or setting it down on boards

FIGURE 6.2 Bowling Stance.

FIGURE 6.3 Arm Action (Approach).

APPROACH

Skill	Cue	Alternate Cue	Common Error
Leg Action (Figure 6.4)	First step very short Second step medium Third step long Fourth step longest	Each step is a little longer and faster	First step too long
Timing	First step and push away together Second and third steps with down and back swing Fourth step with forward swing and delivery	Keep ball swinging and feet walking	Feet finishing before arm swing

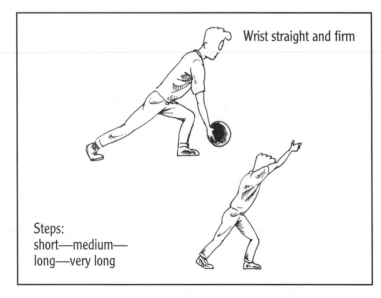

Wrist straight and firm

Steps:
short—medium—
long—very long

FIGURE 6.4 Leg Action (Approach) and Delivery.

DELIVERY			
Skill	**Cue**	**Alternate Cue**	**Common Error**
Straight Ball	Wrist straight and firm (Figure 6.4)	Thumb at 12 o'clock position	Arm rotation right or left
	Release ball as arm passes vertical and starts upward	Trajectory like airplane landing 3 to 4 feet beyond foul line	Dropping or setting ball on approach before foul line
			Holding ball too long causes you to loft ball
	Follow-through in straight upward swing	Arm points in direction you want ball to go	Stopping arm action on release of ball
	Shoulders stay square (parallel) to foul line		Body rotates clockwise on ball of left foot
Hook Ball	Cup the palm	Thumb at 10:30 position	
	Hand stays behind ball		Hand on side of ball
	Thumb comes out first (ball spins counterclockwise)	Deliver ball with finger only	Spin like a top
	On release flip the fingers and shake hands	Release with the V form	
	Follow through in straight upward swing		
Leg Action	Lower the body during third and fourth steps	Bend knees to smoothly lower body at end of approach	Bouncy up-and-down action
	Decelerate fourth step	Left foot steps and slides to a stop	Loss of balance from too quick a stop
	Keep back foot in contact with floor	Don't spin out	Poor timing results in picking up back foot and clockwise body rotation
	Left knee and foot point toward pins	Keep facing target	Body rotation

USE OF ARROWS

Skill	Cue	Alternate Cue	Common Error
Using Arrows	Easier to hit a target 15 feet away than one 60 feet away	Focus eyes and attention on aiming points (arrows)	Looking at pins
Three Basic Positions			
Strike	Second arrow from right	10 boards in from right edge	
Right-Side Spare	Third arrow from left	15 boards in from left	
Left-Side Spare	Third arrow from right	15 boards in from right	
Aim of Eyes (Strike)	Second arrow from right	10 boards in from right side	Bowling down center of lane
Placement of Feet (Strike)	Left toe on second dot board from right	Third dot from right at foul line	
Use of Arrows (Spare)	Use one of three basic positions; move start position one board left to move ball contact three boards right; move feet one board right to move ball contact three boards left	1-inch change in starting position equals 3-inch change in ball contact point	
Aim of Eyes (Spare)	Left-side spares (7 pin, etc.): same starting position as strike ball—aim over third arrow from right Right-side spares (10 pin): third arrow from right		Bowling down left side of lane

USE OF ARROWS

Skill	Cue	Alternate Cue	Common Error
Placement of Feet (Spare)	Left-side spares: same as strike starting position; make slight adjustments right or left to change ball contact point Right-side spares: left foot four boards in from far left edge of lane	Left toe on second dot from right	
Splits	Use same arrows as spares; adjust starting position slightly right or left to change contact point of ball		
Adjustments *Leaving Spares*	Are you hitting your target on arrow? If no, hit target If yes, keep same target; move starting position one to three boards in direction you're missing the pocket		Not hitting target on arrow Moving too far or changing target

SCORING

Skill	Cue	Alternate Cue	Common Error
Open Frame	Count pins you knock over	Pin count	
Spares	Score 10, plus pin count from next ball	Maximum 20 points	
Strikes	Score 10, plus pin count from next two balls	Maximum 30 points	

Chapter 7

Cross-Country Running

INTRODUCTION

Coaches sometimes get too caught up in the mechanics of running. If coaches would block out the upper body and see what the legs are doing, they would often find that runners have good mechanics from the waist down. Runners are doing what feels good to them. Remember that the runner is propelled along the ground by the legs, not the arms, head, or hands. Arms are for balance. The reasons why runners may not have perfect mechanics could be a leg-length discrepancy, spine curvature, or an individual structural difference (people are wired differently).

You are fooling around with nature when trying to make major changes in the mechanics of runners. The more people run, the more they will develop efficient and economical running styles. Relaxation and running economy are the keys. It also helps to inherit good genes.

SKILLS LISTED WITH CUES

In this chapter we have structured cues for the following: runner's cues, uphill running, downhill running (short steep hills, gradual hills), corners, building striders, striders, preparation on the race course, prerace routine, start of race, racing strategy, postperformance routines, junior and senior high school mileage, and scoring.

TIPS

1. As much training as possible should be done on grass, trails, and soft surfaces to avoid injuries. This point is especially important if you are going to be racing on grass.
2. Watch runners through binoculars and give detailed observations into a dictaphone. Edit tape for unproductive, emotional comments before having runners listen to it.
3. After race have runners comment into a dictaphone about how they felt and their performance level (positive and negative things about it).
4. Have runners hydrate well before, during, and after practice and races.

EQUIPMENT TIPS FOR COACHES

1. Dictaphone (microcassette)
2. Good pair of binoculars
3. Stopwatch
4. Video camera and operator

EQUIPMENT TIPS FOR RUNNERS

1. Spiked racing shoes
2. Flat training shoes
3. Water, towels

TEACHING IDEAS

1. *Warm-up ritual/routine:* Jog about 1 mile on grass with flat shoes, stretch out approximately 10 minutes, jog about 1 mile, building striders 2 to 4 miles. Make the warm-up similar to race preperformance ritual/routine.
2. *Two workouts per day:* Start with daily early *morning runs* about 2 to 3 miles during training season at 79% to 80% of runner's top speed.
3. *Afternoon workouts, M-W-F:* A hard workout might include a long, hard run on Monday, a gradual uphill distance run on Wednesday, and fartlek training on a grass "hilly" park on Friday. *T-Th-S:* Easy workouts to finish running mileage for week's total.
4. *Hard/easy weeks (20/30—20 miles one week, 30 miles next week):* Gradually build up mileage. Avoid overtraining as it causes injuries.

FYI

For further information and special help, consult the following organization:

Road Runners Club of America (RRCA)—National association of nonprofit running clubs
1150 South Washington Street, Suite 250
Alexandria, VA 22314–4493
Phone: (703) 836–0558
Fax: (703) 836–4430

1. Provides information on local clubs.
2. Dedicated to promoting long-distance running as a competitive sport and as healthful exercise.
3. Mission to represent and promote the common interest of its member clubs.
4. Running clubs join the RRCA for a modest annual fee and receive a range of programs and services in return. Services include nonprofit tax exempt status, liability insurance, equipment insurance, and others.
5. Provides running books, videos, a curriculum guide for teachers and coaches, and a program guide for parents and children.

RUNNER'S CUES			
Skill	Cue	Alternate Cue	Common Error
Relaxation (Figure 7.1)	Work on drills to relax face, jaw, neck, shoulders, arms, and hands	Repeat the word *relax* or use other predetermined cues	Tensing: Face Jaw Neck Shoulders Arms Hands
Breathing (Figure 7.2)	Belly breathing	Pouch stomach out as you breathe in	Side aches caused by breathing too fast and high in chest

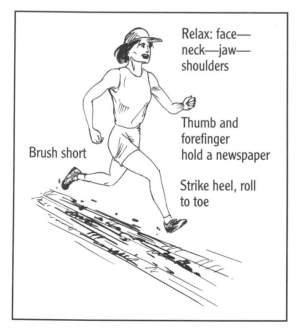

FIGURE 7.1 Distance Runner's Cues.

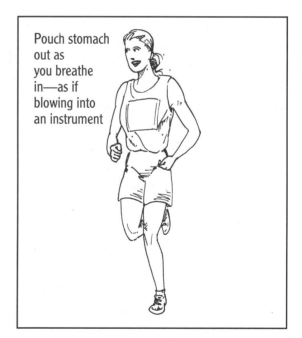

FIGURE 7.2 Correct Breathing Pattern for Runners.

HILL RUNNING

Skill	Cue	Alternate Cue	Common Error
Uphill (Figure 7.3)	Short quick strides	Quickly get feet back to touching ground	Overstriding
	Compact stride contained within oneself		
	Run on forefoot		
	May lean forward depending on steepness of hill		
	Maintain the hill and power over the crest of the hill		Slowing down at the top of the hill
Downhill			
Short Steep Hills	Brake to avoid falling and/or gaining too much speed	There is a high risk of falling	Gaining too much speed

Quickly get feet back to touching ground

Run on forefoot

Short quick strides

FIGURE 7.3 Running Uphill.

HILL RUNNING

Skill	Cue	Alternate Cue	Common Error
Downhill (*cont.*)			
Short Steep Hills (cont.)	Use a heel-first running stride	Heel first, braking action is on heels	
	Shorter braking stride	Short quick steps	Overstriding
	Arms come out further away for balance		Arms too close to body
	Power down the hill with shorter steeper hills	This type of running stride takes a lot of energy from the runner	
Gradual Hills	Make body perpendicular to hill	Longer strides	Overstriding
	Keep hips forward		
	Swing out arms away from body for balance	Arms in rhythm	
	Place foot under center of gravity		
	Let gravity work with you	Free rolling type of action	
	Maintain body balance		

STRIDERS

Skill	Cue	Common Error
Building Strider		
1–50 Meters	Start from jog, go into a good pace by 50 meters	Sprinting too soon
50–80 Meters	Accelerate to 80% of full speed	Accelerating over 80% of full speed
80–100 Meters	Smooth transition to acceleration and then to deceleration	Decelerating too quickly

STRIDERS

Skill	Cue	Common Error
Strider *Distance*	50 to 100 meters total distance Begin slowly, but by 50 meters athlete is at 80% speed	Athlete is over 80% speed

RACE COURSE PREPARATION

Skill	Cue	Alternate Cue	Common Error
Knowing the Course	Go over course before race		Not taking time to go over course; arriving too late
	Walk or run course alone	Have teammates run course alone—helps them focus	Running the course with team instead of individually; good for team unity, but all may not focus on course
	Have a tentative plan		
	Know where crucial hills and blind spots are on course		Daydreaming during course

RITUALS

Skill	Cue	Alternate Cue	Common Error
Prerace	If the coach has done job, should be no no coaching	When countdown starts for the athlete, do not interfere	Pep talks to team and individuals just before race

RITUALS			
Skill	**Cue**	**Alternate Cue**	**Common Error**
Prerace *(cont.)*	Athlete knows what is expected early in week	Example of ritual: Athlete finds quiet spot; makes restroom stop; jogs about 1 mile; stretches alone; makes restroom stop; puts on spike shoes or racing flats; jogs; 2 to 6 building striders; walks or jogs 5 minutes	
	Warm up 40 to 60 minutes before competition		
Warm-Up for Hot Days	A shorter warm-up is needed		
	Be sure to hydrate well all day		
	Warm up in shade if possible		
Warm-Up for Cold Days	A longer warm-up is needed		
	Don't forget to hydrate		

RACING			
Skill	**Cue**	**Alternate Cue**	**Common Error**
Start	Both arms down		Both arms up
	Dominant leg back		Weakest leg back
	Most weight on back foot		Weight even or too much on front leg
Leg Action	Push off back foot first		Forgetting to push with back leg first
Arm Action	Arms come up to protect yourself at the crowded start		Left arm forward and left leg forward

RACING			
Skill	**Cue**	**Alternate Cue**	**Common Error**
Strategy			
Beginning of a Race	Begin a race significantly fast, in order to gain good position	Brigham Young University women's cross-country concept:	Getting behind at start
	Maintain good early position	Be near front	Going out too fast for too long
		Position	
		Control breathing	High quick breathing
		Find key people position	
		Fast and relaxed	
	Draw into oneself, the sport, and opponent	"I feel strong"	Responding to harassment by spectators
Tactics During Race (Figure 7.4)	Catch someone and pass 'em	Catch someone and beat 'em	Not focusing on a runner or group of runners ahead of you to pass
	Don't get into no-man's-land	Don't run alone; stay with with group	Not staying with the pack or another runner
	Focus on the runner in front of you by imagining a rope between her and you and she is slowly pulling you in		
	Hills present opportunities to pass runners	Pass runners after a turn, over a hill, or through trees	Don't attack or charge up hills; it's not energy efficient

Don't get into no-man's-land

Catch someone and pass 'em

Catch someone and beat 'em

FIGURE 7.4 Strategy During a Race.

RACING			
Skill	**Cue**	**Alternate Cue**	**Common Error**
Strategy *(cont.)* *Tactics During Race (cont.)*	Blind spots are effective for 20 to 50 yards when runners cannot be seen	Accelerate coming out of a turn, over a hill, or through trees to discourage other runners	
	Use of groups is helpful to break opposing groups (extended acceleration of 100 to 200 yards)		
Postperformance Ritual	Flexibility exercises	It is crucial to work muscles and ligaments through a range of motion	Overtraining runners
	Jogging, very easy running (no acceleration, flat terrain, training shoes)	A cool-down will help recovery	Distance over 2 miles
			Overuse injuries from lack of proper adaptation time

MILEAGE		
Skill	**Cue**	**Common Error**
Junior High Distance Races	1 to 2 miles At the junior high level, 1 mile can be a long distance	Overtraining runners Distance over 2 miles Injuries from lack of proper adaptation time
High School Distance Races	2 to 3 miles Cross-country distance is 3 miles/ 5 kilometers	Overtraining runners School schedules often require two competitions per week. If this is done all season, it may be too much racing. Injuries from lack of proper adaptation time

SCORING			
Skill	**Cue**	**Alternate Cue**	**Common Error**
Team Scoring	Only the first five runners on team score Rest of runners influence other scores Sixth- and seventh-place runners don't affect their team's score but do affect the scores of other teams All other runners in the race do not figure in the tallying of points	Runners are given points according to their place Top five runners' points are added up Team with lowest score wins	

Chapter 8

Cycling—Mountain Biking

INTRODUCTION

Mountain biking is a relatively new fitness sport that is becoming extremely popular. Mountain biking requires anaerobic and aerobic power as terrain varies.

Mountain biking requires a variety of skills to cope with obstacles such as rocks, logs, switchbacks, creeks, ditches, holes, tire ruts, animal crossings, washouts, shale, and so on. The cues in this chapter will help the biker practice safety, learn correct biking technique, have more fun, and experience success more quickly.

SKILLS LISTED WITH CUES

Included in this chapter are cues for the following techniques: buying the correct size bike, body position (feet, seat, upper body while climbing, descending, or riding in rough terrain), pedaling, braking to stop fast or to corner in loose terrain, and shifting under a load.

SAFETY TIPS

1. Statistics show that in the majority of bicycle accidents the rider falls off the bicycle for some reason. The remainder of accidents are collisions with automobiles, fixed objects, and other bicyclists.
2. Check brakes and pads. There shouldn't be so much play in brakes that you have to completely squeeze them before they'll work. Check quick releases; make sure they are tight (by the way, that's what holds the wheels on).
3. Check all cables (frayed cables could cause a serious accident).
4. Check bottom bracket. Grab the crank arm, not the pedal, and move it from side to side. If there is any play, the bike needs adjustment. The wheels should be checked in the same way. Any play in these needs to be adjusted immediately.
5. Check lock on front brake. Rock it forward and backward. If there is any play in the head set, get it adjusted immediately, or it can be expensive.
6. Every bike, no matter how much it is ridden, needs a checkup every year. If something is wrong with your bike get it checked more often.
7. Keeping a bike clean may avoid the expense of unnecessary maintenance.

Padded gloves	Two water bottles
Snacks and cut-up fruit in plastic bags	Frozen juice packs
Binoculars	Tire kit

FIGURE 8.1 Equipment Needed for Mountain Bikers on Trails.

EQUIPMENT TIPS

1. The first and most important equipment needed is the helmet. (See recommendation in FYI and Figure 8.1 for all equipment recommendations.)
2. Padded biking gloves are best because they provide safety and cushioning during a ride and during a wreck (the palms usually hit first in a wreck); they also provide better friction between hand and grip, especially when hands are moist.
3. Lightweight biking components are suggested.
4. Gears are a matter of personal preference and riding terrain. Counsel with local bike dealers for area specifications.
5. Two water bottles. Precaution: hydrate well even when you don't feel like drinking. Bikers are not aware of how much water is lost.
6. Snacks: hard candies to keep mouth moist; fruit and other foods cut into bite-size pieces and put in plastic sandwich bags; "gorp" for long rides—raisins, peanuts, and the like; and chocolate caramel malted bars (two-thirds of their calories come from carbohydrates).
7. Frozen juice and fruit drinks in aluminum foil packets.
8. Binoculars, which improve view and enjoyment of outdoors.
9. Lightweight jacket.
10. Biking shorts (optional): not only increase comfort but also increase circulation.
11. The following items should be carried on every ride in your backpack or bag: tire repair kit and chain breaker, spare tube, portable air pump, patch kit, tire levers, a quarter for phone calls.
12. Toe clips: optional but highly recommended. They will keep the foot in the proper position on the pedal and will allow force to be applied while both pushing down and pulling up on the same pedal, a motion known as pedaling in circles (see cue for riding uphill).

TEACHING IDEAS

1. Start in a parking lot and become familiar with the bike and its gears. Practice shifting; get the feel of what is easy and hard. Practice turns and braking. Move to wide, flat dirt roads, then to a wide dirt hill with a gradual incline.
2. Practice braking techniques. The rear one comes on first. Practice on dirt roads so when you get on the trail it is not a drastic transition.
3. Practice smooth transitions while shifting, especially under a load (riding uphill).
4. Technical riding: Provide rocks or cones, and ride between them. Such practice helps riders know where the front and rear wheels are. Make different trails. This drill helps riders know when they hit a rock or cone, or when they do it right. This particular drill will teach where the front and rear wheels are on the trail. The front and back wheels are not the same.
5. Practice braking downhill as well as going downhill.
6. Technical skills can be practiced all the time.
7. Once you get the feel of the bike on these terrains, then you can move to rougher terrains and sharper turns, with hills and other different situations.
8. Practice these basic skills on varying types of terrains.

FYI

For further information and special help, consult the following organizations and source:

U.S. Cycling Federation
One Olympic Plaza
Colorado Springs, CO 80909
Phone: (719) 578–4581
Fax: (719) 578–4956

Bicycling Magazine
New Rider Network
Box 6075
Emmaus, PA 18098

Provides rules of the trail and a free 40-page book especially for newcomers who want to get started right on a bike.

Bell Sports
P.O. Box 13349
Denver, CO 80201–3349
Phone: 1–800–456–Bell

Provides information regarding helmets.

1. Bell will replace your helmet for only $15.00 if you write and explain the crash.
2. With this information Bell can do research on actual crashes.
3. A Bell helmet has many air vents, permitting hot air to be replaced by cool air while riding. This ventilation reduces the risk of heat exhaustion.
4. A Bell helmet goes down lower and protects the occipital lobe of the brain, which is responsible for sight and other critical functions.

Sloane, E. (1988). *The complete book of cycling*. New York: Simon & Schuster.

BIKE SIZE

Skill	Cue	Common Error
Upper Body	Good cockpit space Seat to handlebar distance is comfortable	If space is too small, hunchback occurs. If space is too large you end up in a stretched-out position, causing upper back and neck to get sore or stiff.
Legs	Stand over bar	Bike is too big. When riding up steep hill front wheel comes up. Bike also corners poorly.
	Ride a few sizes	A bike that is too small can be uncomfortable because you bend over too far.
	Get smallest bike you are comfortable riding	Bike too big, high center, "ouch"
Seat Height	At bottom of stroke knees slightly bent	Too high: knees are hyperextended, or hip rocking occurs

BODY POSITION

Skill	Cue	Common Error
Feet	Ball of foot over axle of pedal	Foot too far forward, pedal under arch
Seat Position	Position seat so that when knees and legs are at 3 and 9 o'clock, seat is slightly behind ball of foot and pedal axle	
Upper Body	About 60% of body weight should be over rear wheel and 40% over front wheel	

UPHILL—DOWNHILL—ROUGH TERRAIN RIDING

Skill	Cue	Common Error
Riding Uphill	Balance weight 60% to 70% over back wheel and 30% to 40% over front wheel to keep traction in back	Not enough weight on front wheel will cause front wheel to come off ground
	Shift weight to middle to keep front wheel down so that you do not lose traction in loose dirt	
	Pedal in circles, using both a pulling and pushing action on each pedal	Using only a pushing action
Riding Downhill	Move back on seat and down	Sitting too far forward on seat causes flying over handlebars
	Hold seat with upper thigh	
	Watch ahead; pick a path (Figure 8.2)	

Watch ahead; pick a path

Move back on seat

Hold seat with upper thigh

Stay low

FIGURE 8.2 Body Position for Riding Downhill.

UPHILL—DOWNHILL—ROUGH TERRAIN RIDING

Skill	Cue	Common Error
Riding in Rough Terrain	Power through corner Keep rear wheel behind you Relax, go with the flow Stutter-step; get dominant foot in front toe position Be like a shock absorber Soak up the bumps with knees and arms like a sponge Let bike float over things Straddle saddle, stand on pedals Avoid hitting obstacles with pedal	Too stiff; cannot let knees, elbows, body flow to absorb bumps

PEDALING—BRAKING—SHIFTING

Skill	Cue	Common Error
Pedaling	Mountain cadence at a spin of about 80 RPM Ride smarter not harder	Usually too slow, which lugs your motor
Braking		
To Stop Fast	Scoot buttocks back Pedal at 3 and 9 o'clock position Squeeze both brakes	Sitting too far forward, weight shifts forward Squeezing one brake
	Keep both wheels on the ground Keep tires from skidding	When squeezing both brakes, body position is too far forward
To Corner in Loose Terrain	Control slide of rear wheel for faster shape cornering Move weight to inside Pedal through corner	Failing to make corner, slowing way down, losing control of front wheel, and turning too hard
Shifting under a Load	Anticipate shift Shift front gear first; fine tune with smaller gears Give pedals a hard push for $\frac{1}{2}$ stroke; then ease off and shift	Waiting before cadence slows before shifting Not easing off pedal prior to shifting

CLEANING THE BIKE

Skill	Cue	Common Error
Drive Train	Remove dirt and grease	Using water
	Use oil-based lubricants	
Steps to Clean	Turn bike upside down, balance on handlebars to clean	Resting bike on kickstand
Spraying	Spray oil-based lubricant on chain in back cassette while turning pedals backward	Turning pedals forward
	Continue to spray for 3 to 5 seconds	Spraying longer than 5 seconds
	Chain in middle of back gears when spraying	Chain on either end
After Spraying	Grab a rag and place it around bottom part of chain in between the two cassettes	
	Continue pedaling backward; change rag to a clean spot; continue pedaling	Pedaling forward
	Change rag until no more dirt or grease comes off on rag	Using dirty rag
	Take rag and run it between gears trying to remove any excess dirt	
Finish Coat	After removing all dirt and grease, place a finish coat of polytech or dry lube; both are dry lube–based and will protect chain from collecting dirt while riding	Not applying a finish coat
Spray	Spray dry lube–based finish coat for one to two complete backward pedal rotations	
Check Chain	Even though a chain looks clean, it usually is not	Not cleaning chain often enough

RULES OF THE TRAIL

Skill	Cue	Common Error
Guidelines		
Ride on Open Trails Only	Respect trail and road closures, private property, and requirements for permits and authorizations	
Leave No Trace	Don't ride when ground will be marred such as on certain soils after it has rained	
	Never ride off trail or skid tires	
	Never discard any object. Pack out more than you pack in	
Control Your Bicycle	Inattention for even a second can cause disaster	
	Excessive speed frightens and injures people	
Always Yield	Make your approach well known in advance to hikers, horseback riders, and other bikers	
	A friendly greeting is considerate and appreciated	
	Stop and walk when horses are present	
Never Spook Animals	Give them extra room and time to adjust to you; running livestock and disturbing wild animals are serious offenses	
	Leave ranch and farm gates as you find them, or as marked	
Plan Ahead	Know your equipment, your ability, and the area in which you are riding, and prepare accordingly	
	Be self-sufficient	
	Keep bike in good repair	
	Carry necessary supplies	

Chapter 9

Cycling—Road Biking

INTRODUCTION

Accomplished riders become highly skilled through countless hours aboard a bike, for there is no substitute for time and mileage. Most have also had some coaching, both formal and informal, which has honed their skills at all levels, especially early in their experience. Remember, cycling isn't fun if you're not in shape or if you lack technique.

Oftentimes cycling skills are learned by trial and error. For example, you purchase a new road bike, strap yourself in for the first time, and feel a little uncomfortable with the new situation. You take the bike for a spin and find yourself faced with narrow roads, sand and gravel on roads, hills, different terrain, traffic, corners, new gears, trying to drink from a water bottle, and so on, not to mention rude drivers. Cyclists could benefit from cues to help them feel more successful with techniques and master the different situations. Following the rules of the road is key to increasing safety when riding in motor vehicle traffic.

SKILLS LISTED WITH CUES

The ideas and cues contained in this chapter are concerned with methods of learning to cycle properly, including buying the correct size of bike, developing correct body position on the bike, pedaling for effective energy transfer (pedaling action, revolutions per minute, and riding in a straight line), cornering (braking, anticipating turns, sharp corners), climbing hills, the transition from climbing to descending, and descending a hill.

TIP

1. Practice bunny hops, corners, and turning.

EQUIPMENT TIPS

1. Purchase road bikes that weigh less than 24 pounds.
2. The first road bike should cost about $700 to $900.
3. Clipless pedals are easier to twist out of (twist sideways), but more energy efficient.
4. It is harder to get feet out of strapped pedals. Coast to 5 MPH, practice pulling feet out of pedals. Caution: the rider will tip over sideways if the foot is not pulled out in time.
5. Purchase riding shoes that are comfortable and have stiff soles. The bottom of the foot is like a platform that gives you more energy transfer.

TEACHING IDEAS

1. Stretch before and after riding, especially the hamstrings, quadriceps, and calf muscles.
2. Start slow and progress. As your miles increase, increase the number of days. Add another day up to five or six days a week. Take Wednesday and Sunday off. Learn to listen to your body.
3. Each rider is different when he or she starts putting in mileage. Ride for fun! Ride more days rather than taking one long ride.
4. Technical skills: practice bunny hopping in a parking lot. Use lines in a parking lot to hop the bike or jump with both wheels over an obstacle. Lift up on the handlebars, jump over the line or bunny hop over the line by raising both wheels. This drill helps the rider when faced with an unexpected pothole or other obstacle in the road. Learn to ride with a group; doing so improves technical skills and enhances intensity of the workouts.
5. There are two types of spinning drills—muscle and spinning cadence. Always spin at a constant cadence.
6. Spin to win! Try to keep the same pace on long rides. For example, if you are laboring and spinning too slowly, drop from 8th gear to 6th gear for a 10-speed bike, and 16th gear to 12th gear for a 20-speed bike. Spinning faster causes less pressure on the legs, but the rider maintains the same speed.
7. Practice positioning down hills. Tuck in behind the stem. Every time you run out of pedal, practice getting very aerodynamic.
8. Practice sprinting: come up out of the saddle into a standing position, hands hanging on to brake hoods and handlebars. Rock bike side to side, keep the wheels in line, and stay in a straight line or hold your line. Avoid wheels zigzagging.

FYI

For further information and special help, consult the following organizations and sources:

U.S. Cycling Federation
One Olympic Plaza
Colorado Springs, CO 80909
Phone: (719) 578–4581
Fax: (719) 578–4956

Bicycling Magazine
New Rider Network
Box 6075
Emmaus, PA 18098

Provides a free 40-page book especially for newcomers.

Bell Helmets (see FYI, Chapter 8)

Burke, E. (1986). *The science of cycling*. Champaign, IL: Human Kinetics.

Doughty, T. (1983). *The complete book of competitive cycling*. New York: Simon & Schuster.

BIKE SIZE

Skill	Cue	Common Error
Selecting a Bike	Proper bike size is critical when purchasing a bike	
	Stand straddling bike with 2 to 3 inches of crotch clearance	No clearance or too high: 3 to 4 inches off ground

BODY POSITION

Skill	Cue	Common Error
Become More Aerodynamic (Figure 9.1)	Decrease frontal area; keep back flat	Body is big, like a sail
	Get prone with elbows and knees in	
	Wear tight clothing	Wearing baggy clothing
	It takes practice to become comfortable; work 5 to 10 minutes at a time in biking position	Not holding position
	Hands should hold bar lightly	White knuckles, gripping too tight, wasting energy
	Bend at waist	Back vertical
	Eyes glance ahead	People do not look ahead, and they run into things or the head stays down

FIGURE 9.1 Correct Body Position on Bike.

PEDALING FOR EFFECTIVE ENERGY TRANSFER

Skill	Cue	Common Error
Pedaling Action	Spin, pedal in circles not squares	Mashing and stomping pedals
	Downstroke motion, like scraping mud off your shoes	Pushing hard at bottom of stroke will not do any good, just attempts to lengthen crank action
	Backstroke motion: pick up your feet	Many riders only push on downstroke and fail to apply pressure to pedals all the way around the circle
		Dead time at 6 o'clock or bottom of pedal stroke
Revolutions per Minute (RPMs)	80 RPMs, adults 90 to 120 RPMs, racers	Pedaling too slow, lugging motor, hard on your knees
Riding in a Straight Line	Keep eyes on road 10 to 15 yards ahead	Not looking ahead causes one leg to fight the other and creates a rocking or a bouncing motion that depletes energy
		Keeping eyes focused on front wheel
	Ride straight	Wobbling

CORNERING

Skill	Cue	Common Error
Braking	Assess the speed and do all braking entering corner or curve	Applying brakes while leaning through a corner or curve will cause handling problems
Anticipating Turn	Start wide and head for inner tip or point of turn	Not turning until well into the corner, which slows you down and can be dangerous

CORNERING

Skill	Cue	Common Error
Anticipating Turn *(cont.)*	Visualize the line or path you will travel through the curve and follow it	Following a jerky, changing path
	Lean bike and carve your line through the turn	
	Keep outside pedal down; stand on it to lower center of gravity	Leaning too far into curve, hitting ground with inside pedal
	(Figure 9.2)	Crash!
Sharp Corner	Raise inside pedal to top of pedal stroke	Making sparks while cornering with pedal
		Dragging pedal

Keep outside pedal down; stand on it

Pop inside knee out

Raise inside pedal to top of pedal stroke

FIGURE 9.2   Cornering.

CLIMBING		
Skill	**Cue**	**Common Error**
Breathing	Breathe from stomach like blowing into an instrument	Breathing in chest, short gasping breaths
Sitting Climb	Push butt into saddle and push back on handlebars (squeeze saddle with butt like a leg press)	
	Scoot back on seat; sit hunkered down; helps to use your buttocks' muscles more	Sitting on seat too hard and not standing on pedal
	Choose easy gear	Gear too tight
	Pull up on bars, so you can push harder on the pedals like giving yourself more weight on a scale	
	RPM minimum 50; spin if you can, uphill	Low RPM makes poor recovery
	Get into *your* rhythm	Trying to match someone else's pace
Standing Climb	Stand, lean forward, pull up and down on bars, and rock the bike	
	Make sure your line stays straight	
Transition from Climbing to Descending	Accelerate near top of hill, pick up speed fast	Trying to recover at top of hill Decelerating at crest of hill
	Recovery occurs after descending speed is reached	

DESCENDING		
Skill	**Cue**	**Common Error**
Position for Fast, Steep Descent	When you cannot pedal fast enough, you spin out	
Grip	Grip the handlebars near the stem, hands right next to each other	Hands on end of handlebars
Body Position (Figure 9.3)	Back flat, feet at 3 and 9 o'clock position	Chest up
	Weight on the pedals, knees in	Weight on arms, knees out

FIGURE 9.3   Body Position for Descending.

RULES OF THE ROAD

Skill	Cue	Common Error
Ride on the Right	Always ride on right; go with flow of traffic	Riding in middle of road; going against traffic
	Be predictable; maintain a straight line; change direction without swerving	Swerving back and forth
Hand Signals	Use hand signal when turning same as motorist; when making a right turn, use your right arm to point	Not using hand signal when turning
Stay Alert	Obey all traffic laws	Breaking traffic rules
	Pay attention	Wearing headphones
	Use your eyes and ears as warning devices alerting you to potential hazards	
	Assert yourself	Letting vehicles creep by, forcing biker into parked cars or curb
	Ride defensively	
	Expect a car to pull from side street or turn left in front of you; if you anticipate the worse, it will rarely happen	Daydreaming
What to Wear	Be visible, wear bright colors, and put reflectors and reflective tape on your bicycle	Wearing light colors in daytime
		Wearing dark clothing at night
		Not putting reflective tape on bicycles
Warning Signal from Cyclist	Shout: it's the quickest way to let motorists know you're putting them in danger or to warn inattentive pedestrians you are approaching	Not giving a warning signal
Feet Strapped or Connected to Pedal	Loosen strap, twist foot out of pedal	Leaving foot strapped or not twisting foot out of pedal

EATING AND DRINKING WHILE RIDING

Skill	Cue	Common Error
Rule of Thumb	Drink before you're thirsty and eat before you're hungry	Not drinking or eating before ride Eating too much
Hot, Humid Weather	Take a big swig from water bottle every 15 minutes	Not drinking during ride
Most Popular Food	One banana provides 105 calories of carbohydrates and replaces potassium, an important element lost via sweating	
Storing Food	Best place: rear pocket of jersey	
5–20 Miles; Less than 90 Minutes	Eat a preride meal with lots of carbohydrates	Eating too much and not waiting 30 minutes for food to digest
15–50 Miles; 45 Minutes– 3 Hours		
Avoid Bonking	Do not allow glycogen stores to become depleted; this happens when ride is 2 hours or longer; drink sports drinks	Not eating premeals or snacks
Avoid Dehydration	Loss of body fluids results in fatigue; carry sports drink, 1 bottle Carry water, 1 bottle	Not drinking water or sports drinks
50–100 Miles; 4 Hours Plus	Eat lots of carbohydrate-rich foods in days preceding the event	Failing on long rides due to poor eating habits
Premeal	Eat a big meal a couple of hours before the big ride	Not eating a premeal
Snack During Ride	Bananas, sandwiches with jam, honey, apple butter, etc. Nibble through ride	Eating too much at once
Water During Ride	4 water bottles	3 or fewer water bottles

Chapter 10

Field Hockey

INTRODUCTION

Field hockey is one of the oldest organized team sports played in the United States. Field hockey is a team game played on artificial turf or grass in which players use a curved stick and try to drive a hard-core ball into the opposing team's goal. The tactics are similar to soccer, a more commonly played game in the United States.

Modern field hockey evolved in England in the early 19th century. Originally the game was played exclusively by men. Today the game is played by both men and women on six continents. More than 70 countries are members of the International Hockey Federation. In the United States and Canada, field hockey is primarily considered a women's sport.

Field hockey was introduced in the United States in 1901 by Constance Applebee, an English field hockey player. Field hockey became an Olympic event for men in 1928, and an Olympic event for women in 1980.

SKILLS LISTED WITH CUES

We provide cues for the following skills: grip, dribbling—moving with the ball, push pass, receiving—hitting, aerials (flick throw, low lift), shooting, dodging, and defense skills—marking, covering, tackling, and goaltending.

TIPS

1. Players should first learn the skills of running with the ball.
2. Passing and receiving skills should be taught second.

EQUIPMENT TIPS

1. Shin guards and mouth guards are mandatory at the high school level.
2. Recently made hockey sticks have smaller toes that make stick control easier.
3. Cleats (plastic) should be used on grass; turf shoes should be used on artificial surfaces.

TEACHING IDEAS

1. Running with the ball (dribbling) is the first skill that should be taught. It is best taught with competitive relays using obstacles and with small games where everyone has a ball and is moving the ball constantly.
2. Passing and receiving should be taught second and together. You cannot pass to a teammate unless the teammate receives.
3. The hit should be taught only after the preceding skills have been mastered to some degree. In early games the hit should not be allowed.
4. Field hockey can be played in physical education class and should be played in small groups (four, five, six, or seven on each side). STX markets a field hockey training stick that is very useful in physical education classes.
5. A full game consists of two 30-minutes halves with 11 players on each side, including a goalie, and various combinations of players depending on their skills. The most traditional lineup on a field hockey field would be five attackers, three halfbacks, two fullbacks, and one goalkeeper. Many other player lineups are used (4, 3, 2, 1, 1; 3, 3, 3, 1, 1; etc.). At the introductory level of play smaller games should be incorporated into the teaching session. Small games open up the space, provide more opportunity to play the ball, and make tactics easier to master and see.
6. Training sessions should follow this format:
   - Light jog
   - Stretching
   - Running skills for better movement
   - Ball-control skills
   - Technical skills (passing combos, two-against-one concepts, etc.)
   - Games, cooldown, stretching

FYI

For further information and special help, consult the following organization:

United States Field Hockey Association (USFHA)
One Olympic Plaza
Colorado Springs, CO 80909
Phone: (719) 578–4567

1. The USFHA offers learning packs (sticks and balls).
2. Its youth development committee aids in the development of field hockey in the United States.

GRIP		
Skill	**Cue**	**Common Error**
Position	Lay the stick parallel to feet	Hands together
	Point to the right	Pointing to left
	Pick up with left hand	Picking up with right hand
	Right hand halfway down stick	Left hand halfway down stick
	Hold stick firmly but comfortably	Holding stick too loosely
Left Hand	Left hand is the holding hand/turns stick	
Right Hand	Right hand is the pulling and pushing hand	

DRIBBLING		
Skill	**Cue**	**Common Error**
Moving with the Ball (Figure 10.1)	Ball "glued" to stick	Ball too far in front of stick
	Use small taps for grass play	Hitting not tapping
	Keep ball outside and ahead of right foot for grass play	Right foot behind ball
	Keep ball on the right side at 3 o'clock position for turf play	Wasting dribbles
Strategy	To run with ball	

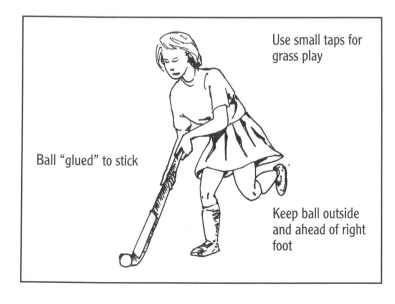

Use small taps for grass play

Ball "glued" to stick

Keep ball outside and ahead of right foot

FIGURE 10.1 The Dribble.

PASSING AND RECEIVING

Skill	Cue	Common Error
Push Pass (Figure 10.2)	Push ball with stick	Wide back swing
	Stick on ball . . . NO contact noise	Stick off ball, tapping or hitting ball
	Firm right hand	Relaxed right hand
	Left wrist pulls stick back	Stiff left wrist
	Short accurate passing	
Strategy	No time to hit ball or shoot	
Receiving	Angle stick slightly forward to deflect ball down	
	Stop ball on stick	Bouncing off stick

Left wrist pulls stick back

Firm right hand

Push ball with stick

Stick on ball

FIGURE 10.2 The Push Pass.

HITTING AND SHOOTING

Skill	Cue	Common Error
Hitting (Figure 10.3)		
Grip	Slide right hand up stick	Forgetting to slide hand up
	Bring hands together on top	Hands too far apart
	Contact ball opposite left foot	Contacting ball off same foot
Driving Action	Hip-to-hip swing like a pendulum	Bending wrists
	Toe of stick up on backswing and up on follow-through	Toe facing grass
	Right hand guides stick in direction of pass	Hand not guiding stick
	Left arm pulls	
	Bend elbow slightly for a relaxed swing	
Strategy	Used for passing and shooting	Bent left arm

Hands together on top of stick

Hip-to-hip swing like a pendulum

Contact ball opposite left foot

FIGURE 10.3   Hitting.

HITTING AND SHOOTING

Skill	Cue	Common Error
Shooting	Variations Follow shot Must be in circle Shots must be on ground or not dangerous	

AERIALS

Skill	Cue	Common Error
Flick Throw	Throwing action Face ball—head, body low Ball between feet (positioning varies) and away from body Toe of stick is extension of hand	
Low Lift	Shovel ball into air, low and gentle Lift the ball up, throwing action Face ball Raise ball slightly—or high depending on what you are trying to do	
Strategy	Used for shooting at close range, penalty, strokes, lifting ball to cover a big distance Used for lifting ball over a defender's stick	

DEFENSE		
Skill	**Cue**	**Common Error**
Footwork	Balance	
	Ability to change direction quickly	
	Drop	
	Approach attacker with control and balance	
	Break down steps	
	Stay in front space	
	Stick defense at 10–2 o'clock position	
Dodges	Get out of the way!	Backing into the defender
	Execute dodge outside of defense playing distance	Anticipating too late or too early
	Execute dodge right off dribble	Stalling
	Accelerate by defender, cut in behind defender	Constant speed and direction
		Crash! Head-on collision
Techniques	1. Pull to the right, accelerate	Backing into the defender
	2. Pull to the left, accelerate	Backing into the defender
	3. Spin and accelerate, must move away from defender	Backing into the defender
Pressuring Defender		
Marking	Stay between your goal and offensive player	Not anticipating soon enough or focusing on defenders
	"Face to face" with your opponent at all times	Tumbling with backside to opponent, losing concentration
Covering		
Supporting Defender	Either mark dangerous space or take next dangerous attacker	
Covering Defender	Make decisions on dangerous space, decide to make attacks or cover space	

DEFENSE		
Skill	**Cue**	**Common Error**
Tackling	Body low, frontal body position	
	Hands and arms away from the body, body in low position, slide stick in, tackle at 5 o'clock position	
	Block ball hand quick, move away with ball	
Goaltending	Stop ball by making a V with ankles—keep knees together	Feet and knees apart
		Standing straight
	Move by sliding feet across goal mouth	Picking up feet
	Always clear ball to sides	Clearing ball in front of cage
	Stop ball before clearing for better control of direction	Hitting ball before clearing
	Can use either side or tip of boot when clearing	Not focusing on ball

Chapter 11

Flag Football

INTRODUCTION

Contact football is very popular throughout the United States and is increasing in popularity throughout the world. To increase participation and minimize injury, flag football has been introduced as another physical education tool. The purpose of flag football is to make maximum participation and enjoyment possible. The following guidelines may be used as a structure to enhance fitness and participation.

SKILLS LISTED WITH CUES

The cues are for throwing, catching, receiving, ball carrying, running (making a turn, changing direction), punting/kicking, blocking, hiking/centering, defense (run, man-to-man, zone, hatchet), scoring, and rules unique to flag football.

TIPS

1. Show an NFL highlight film to help kick off the unit. Let the players name the team: 49ers, Cowboys, Buffalo Bills, Broncos, Cornhuskers, Sooners. Ownership increases motivation. The greater the investment in the activity, the harder players will work. Call players by names of pro football players.
2. Pregame warm-ups: field-goal-kicking contests, longest-throw contests, and one-on-one drills.

EQUIPMENT TIPS

1. Multicolor Nerf footballs are recommended, or use small footballs. Avoid large, regulation-size leather balls (difficult to throw and catch).
2. Divide the 120-yard field into four sections (30 yards wide, 50 yards long) with cones down the middle. Each team can have seven or eight players.
3. Supply pullover pinnies.
4. Flags with Velcro avoid questions of whether the player was down or not.
5. Flip scorecards are helpful. If players can see a scorecard, they will have added motivation.

TEACHING IDEAS

1. Seven on each team (everybody gets a chance to participate).
   Offensive team: one quarterback, two running backs, two receivers, one center (eligible for catching), one tight end. (Option: rotate players every five plays.)
2. Defensive team: two cornerbacks, four linebackers (two inside, two outside), one free safety.
3. Each team is given 10 offensive and 10 defensive plays, rotating every five plays between offense and defense.
4. Modified scoring for offense (the object is to score points and have fun):
   - Designate scoring zones with cones. Place the cones 5/10/15 yards apart.
   - Points are scored for completed passes in designated zones.
   - Player cannot advance ball more than one zone.
   - Receiver must catch ball in touchdown zone for 6 points (no advancing allowed).

1 point	0–5 yards
2 points	5–10 yards
3 points	10–15 yards
6 points	16+ yards

5. Modified scoring for defense:

1 point	Incomplete pass
2 points	Sack (quarterback has to throw ball within 4 seconds)
3 points	Intercepted pass
1 point	Offensive pass interference
6 points	Touchdown

6. Adapt the game so there is more than one forward pass in a play. This gives students more opportunities to participate and score.
7. If interference happens on last play, offense has option to replay down.

FYI

For further information and special help, consult the following organization:

National Football League
410 Park Avenue
New York, NY 10022
Phone: (212) 758–1500

THROWING		
Skill	**Cue**	**Common Error**
Stance	Stand sideways	Feet and stomach facing the target
Grip (Figure 11.1)	Grab top of ball like holding a soda pop can sideways or making a C Finger pads hold laces	Grabbing middle of ball Palm holding ball
Leg Action	Take a short to medium step	Overstriding, high stepping, or taking no steps
Arm Action	Stretch arm way back, make an L Whipping action with wrist (palm out) Index finger responsible for the spin on the ball Palm out at point of release Nose of ball should travel slightly up	Taking ball behind head No snap of wrist Palm turning in Nose of ball in any other position
Release	Picture an eye on right and left front shoulders and on right and left knees; when these four checkpoints on body face target, release ball	

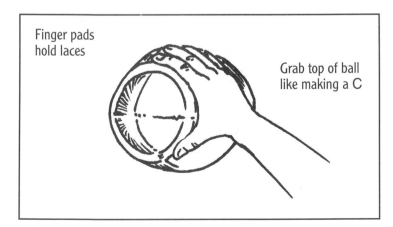

Finger pads hold laces

Grab top of ball like making a C

FIGURE 11.1   Grip for Throwing the Football.

CATCHING AND RECEIVING

Skill	Cue	Common Error
Above the Waist (Figure 11.2)	Make diamond or triangle with forefingers and thumbs; look through the diamond or triangle	Hands apart, palms face sky
	Thumbs in	
Below the Waist (Figure 11.3)	Touch pinkies	Hands apart
	Thumbs out	
	Fingers collapse around the ball like a butterfly net or a Venus fly trap	Hands are like a wall (no collapse)
	Elbows should act as shock absorbers on ball contact	Stiff arms
	Quiet hands/soft hands	
Coaching Point	Diamond	Wrong sequence
	Collapse fly trap	Squeeze ball too soon
	Shock absorber	

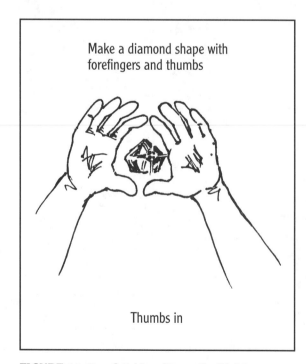

Make a diamond shape with forefingers and thumbs

Thumbs in

FIGURE 11.2 Catching Above the Waist.

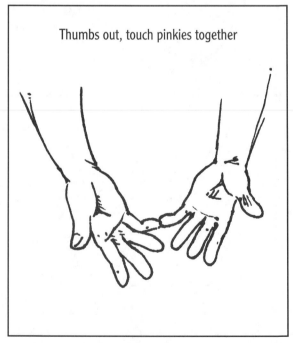

Thumbs out, touch pinkies together

FIGURE 11.3 Catching Below the Waist.

BALL-CARRYING TECHNIQUE

Skill	Cue	Common Error
Tuck Away After Catch (Figure 11.4)	Tuck ball into four pressure points REEF (four pressure points) 　Rib cage (stuff ball into rib cage) 　Elbow (tuck elbow in) 　Eagle claw (spread fingers over point of ball) 　Forearm (cover ball)	Ball not on one of four pressure points Carrying like a loaf of bread

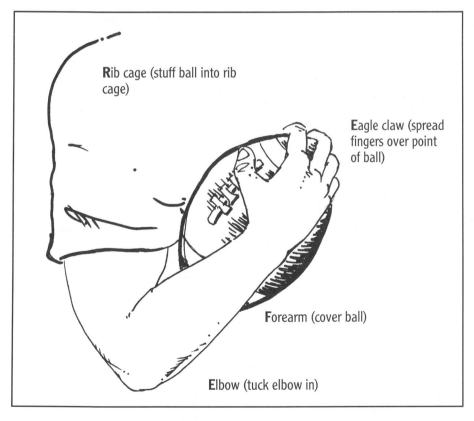

FIGURE 11.4　Ball Carrying Technique—REEF (Four Pressure Points).

RUNNING STRATEGIES

Skill	Cue	Common Error
Fundamentals	Stay light on feet	Planting your heel
	Feet off the ground	
	Run on balls of feet, like a ballerina, smooth and controlled so feet can spin	Feet coming out from underneath, jerky and uncontrolled
		Planting heels can cause knee injury
	Run like a Ferrari race car (low to ground)	Running like a semi (top heavy) can injure ribs
Running Down Sideline (Figure 11.5)	SOAPS: Switch outside arm position	
	Running down right sideline, carry ball in right hand	
	Running down left sideline, carry ball in left hand	

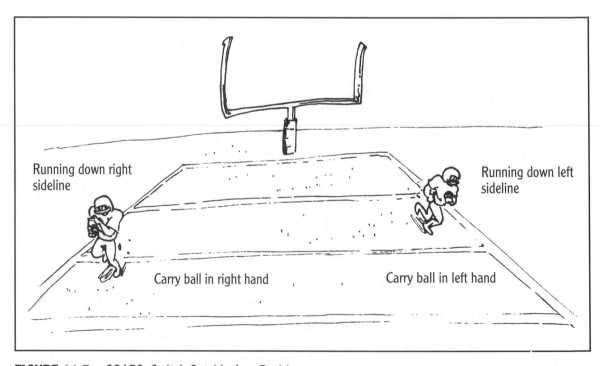

FIGURE 11.5   SOAPS: Switch Outside Arm Position.

RUNNING STRATEGIES

Skill	Cue	Common Error
Change in Direction	Cut off with your lateral foot	Cutting off medial foot causes one to slip
Making a Turn	Make a tight turn	Making a wide turn
	Keep the turn tight	Keeping angle of turn loose
	"Shawn Turner," receiver, Utah State University	

PUNTING/KICKING

Skill	Cue	Common Error
Catch Ball	Catch the ball first (see catching cues)	Fumbling the ball
Grip (Figure 11.6)	Grab end of ball, laces up	Grabbing middle of football
	Make a V with thumb and index finger (laces point straight down the middle of V)	
	Point ball slightly inward and down	Pointing ball straight
	Ball locked on dominant hip	Holding ball in front, not on hip

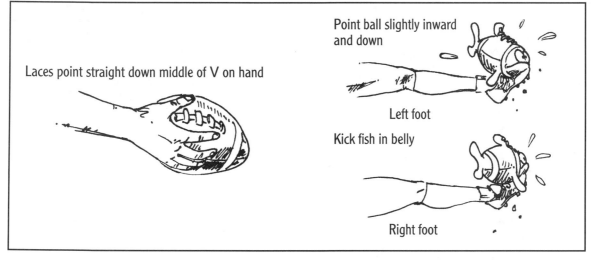

FIGURE 11.6   Punting the Football—Grip and Kicking Action.

PUNTING/KICKING

Skill	Cue	Common Error
Steps into Kick	Walk a balance beam	Not walking straight
Dominant Hand	As you slide the ball along a table, extend dominant hand straight	
	Ball is contacted at edge of table	Dropping ball before kicking
Nondominant Hand	Nondominant hand is a saw guide (hand on side of ball)	Grabbing ball with both hands
	Lock leg and curl toes under	Bending knee and flexing ankle
Kicking Action (Figure 11.6)	Focus on laces and kick a fish in the belly	Slapping at ball or kicking on side
Approach Strategies	Hip to be square	Hips not square to target; rockin' and rollin'

BLOCKING

Skill	Cue	Common Error
Techniques	Sit on heels/sit on a chair	Weight is forward
	Arm hangs	Too much weight on hands
	Hot feet/choppy feet	Stopping feet and lunging
	Mirror the opponent	Not keeping with opponent
	Bust a door open with shoulder and forearm	Using any other parts for blocking
	Push a car uphill	

HIKING OR CENTERING

Skill	Cue	Common Error
Long Snap, 12–14 yards	Sit on heels	
	Pyramid base	
	Cock the trigger (rotate ball clockwise with wrist in flexed position)	Slow snap
	Extend hips and knees like getting kicked in the butt	Generating power with arms
	Focus on punter's belt	Not looking at target
	Reach for belt (palms out)	No follow-through
Shotgun Formation	Same cues as long snap, less force	
Direct Snap (Quarterback Under Center)	While snapping turn ball $\frac{1}{4}$ turn	Not turning ball

DEFENSIVE STRATEGIES

Skill	Cue	Common Error
Techniques	Pedaling bike backward staying on toes	Falling backward
	High knees backward, quick and choppy	Falling backward
		Inability to change direction quickly
	Look through receiver to quarterback	Inability to locate ball
Running Strategy	Grapevine or crossover	Poor hip rotation
Man to Man	Play inside out	Getting beat to inside (letting receiver get inside position)
	Force opponent outward	
Zone	Play outside arm	Receiver able to turn ball upfield for more yardage
	Funnel toward center	
Hatchet	Use arm closest to ball as a hatchet to make opponent miss ball	Receiver not stripped of ball after catch
Coaching Point	Defense is meant to be suppressed; this is mainly an offensive game	

SCORING		
Skill	**Cue**	**Common Error**
Touchdown	6 points	
Field Goal	3 points	
Safety	2 points	
Point after Touchdown	1 point for kick 2 points for running or passing	

RULES UNIQUE TO FLAG FOOTBALL		
Skill	**Cue**	**Common Error**
Players	7 to 11 on a team	
Offensive Team	Three players must be on line of scrimmage	
Defensive Team	No player closer than 3 yards to line of scrimmage	
Game	Four 12-minute periods	
Flag Guarding	Using hand, arms, or clothing or spinning more than once to prevent another player from pulling the flag	
Personal Contact	Enforce rule prohibiting contact with other players	
Illegal Wearing or Pulling of Flag	Illegal for ball carrier to use hands or clothing to hide or prevent opponent from pulling flag	
Dead Ball	Ball is fumbled Scrimmage kick hits ground Ball carrier falls down or flag is pulled	

Chapter 12

Floor Hockey

INTRODUCTION

Floor hockey, a combination of ice hockey, roller hockey, and basketball, is a fast-moving and exciting team game. Floor hockey is strenuous and usually is played on a gym floor. Walls are "alive" (for example, the ball can be played off a wall.) The midcourt line is used as the centerline. Hockey nets are recommended for the goal area. Many teachers are not familiar with this game.

SKILLS LISTED WITH CUES

We provide a few simple guidelines to help the teacher understand the basics of the game and cues for the following skills: grip, stick handling, passing, receiving, and shooting.

TIP

1. A ratio of three balls per player is suggested. This ratio puts a player on task for a longer period of time. No downtime is taken by looking for a ball to do a skill. For example, in shooting drill the player does not have to take time to get the ball out of the net. Other balls will be available.

EQUIPMENT TIPS

1. Use a baseball-size Wiffle ball, and stuff it with rags. Stuffing it takes the bounce out of it. This ball does not hurt players as much, and using stuffed balls promotes the passing aspect of the game (Figure 12.1). Baseball-size Wiffle balls cost 42 to 50 cents each. Instructors can get 100 balls for about $50.00. Manufactured hockey balls and pucks are expensive. They do not roll well and are heavy, characteristics that take away from the team aspect.
2. Use sticks made available by manufacturers. On wood floors use plastic sticks. Wood blades can cause damage to floors.
3. Get broken shafts free from ice hockey leagues, and buy plastic blades at a sporting goods store for about $3.00 or $4.00 apiece (Figure 12.2).

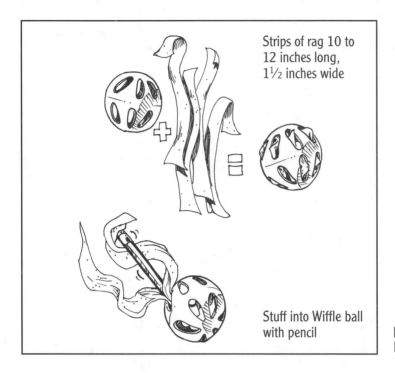

FIGURE 12.1   Modified Floor Hockey Balls.

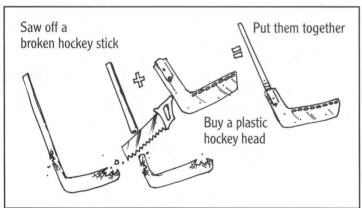

FIGURE 12.2   Modified Hockey Sticks.

TEACHING IDEAS

Rules and skills are exactly the same as ice hockey.

1. Six players: one goalkeeper (stops shots with stick, feet, or hands), one center, two defensive players (left and right), and two offensive players (left and right wings). Positions are interchangeable.
2. Floor hockey, like ice hockey, is a spatial game: that is, player position over the entire court must be maintained for effective offense and defense. To teach beginners the importance of spatial awareness, set up games with fewer players—for example, 5 on 5, 5 on 3, 4 on 3, 3 on 2, or 2 on 1. Students learn basic strategies faster when they have more opportunities to practice.
3. Build offensive and defensive skills and team play: 1 on 1, 2 on 1, 3 on 0, 3 on 1, 3 on 2, 3 on 3, 4 on 2, 5 on 0, 5 on 2, 5 on 3, 5 on 4, 5 on 5. These numbers do not include the goaltenders.

FYI

For further information and special help, consult the following organizations and sources:

USA Hockey
4965 East Fountain Boulevard
Colorado Springs, CO 80910
Phone: (719) 599–5000
Fax: (719) 599–5994

Olympic training ground for the Amateur Hockey Association of the United States.

Ice hockey books for more drills, rules, and information.

GRIPS

Skill	Cue	Common Error
Right-Handed Player	Hands 6 to 10 inches apart	Hands too close together and grip too tight
	V formed by thumb and forefinger on top	
	Hold stick in front of body	
	Elbows and arms should move freely	
	Hold stick firmly but comfortably	Holding stick too loosely
Player Who Shoots Left	Right hand is top hand; left hand is down shaft (vice versa)	

BALL CONTROL		
Skill	**Cue**	**Common Error**
Stick Handling	Cup the ball with blade	Slapping rather than cupping the ball
	Ball motion stays parallel to foot line	
	Roll wrists/extend arms/soft hands	Gripping too tightly/arms held too close to body
	Head up	
Forehand and Backhand Passing	Eyes focus on target	Not looking at target
	Ball on blade, travels heel to toe	
	Sweep ball	Slapping ball
	Cup the ball with blade	Not cupping ball with stick
	Follow-through low	Short or no follow-through
Forehand and Backhand Receiving	Give with blade at right angle, cup ball with blade	Stick is not perpendicular to direction of incoming ball
	Blade must give to maintain control	Blade is left open allowing ball to bounce over stick
	Soft hands	Wrists are held stiff causing ball to bounce over stick

SHOOTING		
Skill	**Cue**	**Common Error**
Forehand and Backhand Wrist Shot	Pull then push, sweep wrist, roll wrist	Poor wrist action resulting in lack of power
	Cup ball with blade	
	Ball rolls from middle of blade to tip	
	Extend arms away from body	Top hand too close to body, therefore limiting movement
	Transfer weight to front foot	Insufficient weight transfer, causing player to fall away from rather than move toward target
	Follow-through determines height of shot	

Chapter 13

Golf

INTRODUCTION

The game of golf is the fastest-growing sport in the world, and, for a student who has played a satisfying round, it is easy to see why it has become so popular. Golf may be the hardest skill game played today, and it definitely cannot be learned quickly. Three things need to happen with each shot. The golfer must 1) hit the target, 2) shoot the correct yardage, and 3) hit the sweet spot on the club face or hit the ball square on the club face. It takes most recreational golfers years to learn, even naturally gifted athletes. Keeping this fact in mind, teachers should remember to be patient with students, while instructing and encouraging those with a real interest in golf to play as much as possible.

Three to five demonstrations of a golf stroke, associated with one cue phrase, will simplify the learning process and make the skill and stroke more beginner-friendly. Stay with one or two cues until the students are comfortable moving on.

For example, if a student thinks "tickle the grass" on the backswing when hitting with a wood, he or she can automatically visualize what needs to be done to make the grass laugh. In other words, keep the club head on the ground longer, rather than lifting it straight up. Doesn't that simplify things?

SKILLS LISTED WITH CUES

This chapter presents teaching cues for the following golf skills: three different grips, approach to the ball, and the basic swing for iron shots. Once the students have mastered these skills, additional cues provide information for golf shots, which include specifics for wood shots, putting, and chipping. Also provided are cues on how to handle sand shots, windy shots, and different golf lies, including downhill, uphill, and low balls. These particular cues are designed for beginning, right-handed golfers, but they can be adapted for left-handed golfers. Through the use of these cues, you and your students can be successful golfers!

TIPS

1. Type the cues on 3″ × 5″ note cards, laminate and hole punch the cards, and place the cards on your bag for quick reference on different shots.

2. It is essential to grasp and ingrain the fundamentals of golf: grip, stance, backswing, through swing, and finish.
3. Good equipment and good fundamentals of golf equal good golf.

EQUIPMENT TIPS

1. Ball differences (colored numbers):
   - *80 compression (all red numbered balls)* suggested for a lady or senior citizen who does not hit the ball very far or has no club-head speed.
   - *90 compression (red and black numbered balls)* suggested for medium to average players, stronger women, and in cold weather for men who hit 100 compression.
   - *100 compression (all black numbered balls)* suggested for stronger men, hot days, fast club-head speed.
2. Standard set of clubs: 1, 3, and 5 woods; 3, 4, 5, 6, 7, 8, and 9 irons; pitching wedge, sand wedge, and putter; and utility clubs: 1 and 2 iron; 4 and 7 wood; and lob wedge.
3. Go to a professional to be fitted for proper club length, proper flex of shaft, and proper lie.
4. Golf shoes with spikes help the golfer stay in the ground and prevent slipping. The author goes barefoot to avoid tearing up the greens.

TEACHING IDEAS

1. Choose clubs beginners can have success with. Clubs that are fairly easy to hit with would include 5, 6, and 7 irons. These clubs can be used to help ingrain the swing. When a player begins to feel comfortable with the irons, progress to the woods.
2. The driving range is a place for beginners to practice the skills of golf. Beginners can become easily frustrated on a golf course. When the beginner can get the ball up in the air with consistency, then it's time to play a round of golf.
3. Putting and chipping are the least difficult skills to learn; however, to keep the feel for the ball one must practice many hours to maintain these skills.
4. Golf is easy to make complex! The simpler we can make it, the better. Stay away from high-tech words. Progress happens when staying with the fundamental skills and basic swing.
5. Setting up a nine-hole golf course on a football field or large grass field is an excellent way to teach scoring and provide a game-like experience (Figure 13.1). Equipment and procedures include the following:
   - Scorecard designed by teacher or picked up at a local golf course.
   - Pencils.
   - Jump rope and cones to mark tee box.
   - For holes use soccer corner flags, or attach flags to dowel sticks and stand the sticks in orange cones with holes in top. Place the flag in the center of a hula hoop. Object of game is to hit ball in hula hoop.
   - Regulation clubs, white Wiffle balls, and tees.
   - Set up nine holes that match the pars on the score card.
   - Use a shotgun tournament start. Have three or four students on each hole. Give each group one wood, a 5 iron, a 7 iron, a 9 iron, a scorecard, and a pencil. On the whistle everybody starts to play.
   - One can play best-ball tournaments and other types. Have fun golfing! Don't forget to try it barefoot.

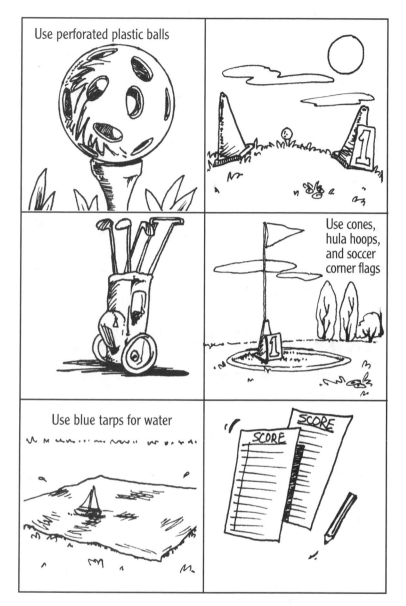

Use perforated plastic balls

Use cones, hula hoops, and soccer corner flags

Use blue tarps for water

SCORE

FIGURE 13.1 Ideas for Modified Golf Equipment and Nine-Hole Golf Course.

6. Have a contest to see who can hit the ball closest to the hole. Tee shots are made from the top of a hill (if hills are not available, tee off level ground) (Figure 13.2).
   • Set up a tee box area and a par-three hole at the bottom of a small hill.
   • Place a hula hoop about 50 yards out from the tee box with a soccer goal marker or flagstick inside the hoop.
   • Place a blue plastic tarp in front of the hole for a water hazard.
   • Provide 7, 8, and 9 irons for the students to use.
   • A teacher, teacher's aide, or a student can place a small flagstick where the closest ball to the large flagstick lands.
   • Each student tries to get her or his shot close to the flagstick. If a student does, the ball is marked with a small flagstick.
   • Closest ball to the hole wins the early bird special.
7. If you don't keep practicing golf, it's very easy to lose your skills. Stay with it.

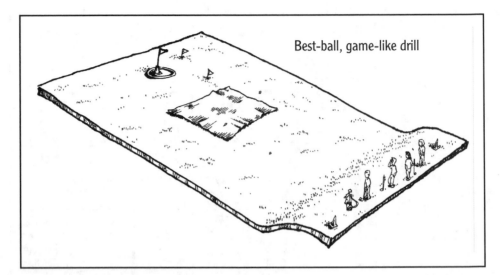
Best-ball, game-like drill

FIGURE 13.2   Early Bird Special Golf Activity.

FYI

For further information and special help, consult the following organization and sources:

Hook a Kid on Golf
2611 Old Okeechobee Road
West Palm Beach, FL 33409
Phone: (407) 684–1141
Fax: (407) 684–2546

PGA professionals at local golf courses.

Fronske, H., Wilson, R., & Strand, B. (1996, November/December). Teaching golf creatively. *Strategies, 10*(2), 32–37.

Hogan, B. (1985). *Five lessons: The modern fundamentals of golf*. New York: Simon & Schuster.

Vroom, J. (1983). *So you want to be a golfer*. San Jose, CA: Vroom Enterprises.

GRIPS			
Skill	Cue	Alternate Cue	Common Error
Overlap (Strongest)	Little finger of right hand rests on index and middle finger	Thumbs go down sides of shaft	Gripping too tightly with right thumb
	Last three fingers of left hand and middle two fingers of right hand are the grippers. Fingers are welded together like Siamese twins.	No pressure with thumb or index finger on club	Gripping top of club—instinctive to grip with thumb and index finger
Hand Position	The V of thumb and index finger of each hand points to right shoulder	Vs point to right shoulder	Gripping too strongly or weakly produces slice or hook
Interlocking	Little finger interlocks with index finger	Used for tiny hands	Little fingers not interlocking
Baseball	No unity between hands, right hand is strong hand of grip	Hold club like a baseball bat	Hands too far apart

APPROACH			
Skill	Cue	Alternate Cue	Common Error
Stance	Sit on tall bar stool	Sit on tall stool	Standing straight up
	Take the seat by bending the knees	Slightly bend knees	Legs stiff or straight
Arms	Make a Y with your arms	Each elbow points at each hip bone	Elbows locked

APPROACH			
Skill	**Cue**	**Alternate Cue**	**Common Error**
Focus of Eyes	Look through the lower part of eyes Chin still	Look through bifocals	Eyes and head tilting down Chin hitting front shoulder during swing
Head	Head needs to be still		

BASIC SWING—IRON SHOTS			
Skill	**Cue**	**Alternate Cue**	**Common Error**
Plane	Vertical plane swinging a Y	Think of shoulders initiating the swing	Horizontal plane, hands initiating the swing
Rhythm	Repeat the words "Slow backswing"		Backswing is too fast or quick
Hips	Accept weight on back leg, like a pitcher winding up	Turn hips back	Hips swaying to side
Weight	Sternum over ball after swing	Chest over ball after swing	Leaning back
Head Position	Head stays still until trailing shoulder forces it up		Looking to see where ball is going
Swing	Hit through ball		
Focus of Eyes	Head stays still until trailing shoulder forces it up		
Slice	Open stance	Outside-to-inside swing	Hands are ahead of ball on impact Swinging too fast on backswing and downswing causing club face to move

BASIC SWING—IRON SHOTS

Skill	Cue	Alternate Cue	Common Error
Hook	Closed stance	Inside-to-outside swing	Hands are behind ball on impact
			Swinging too fast on backswing and downswing causing club face to move

BASIC SWING—WOOD SHOTS

Skill	Cue	Alternate Cue	Common Error
Stance (Figure 13.3)	Front foot lines up with ball		Ball lined up with back foot or middle of stance
Tee Ball	Top half of ball should be above club face		Ball teed up too high or low

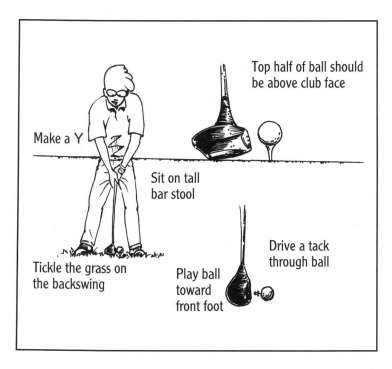

FIGURE 13.3 Stance and Swing for Wood Shot.

BASIC SWING—WOOD SHOTS

Skill	Cue	Alternate Cue	Common Error
Swing	Tickle grass on back swing	Stay low	Wood face comes up too soon
	Emphasize *slow* backswing		Hurrying the take-away swing
	Smooth rhythm swing		
	Drive tack through ball		
	Sweep the ball off tee		Hitting at down angle
Follow-Through	Belt buckle faces hole		Left hip faces hole
Focus of Eyes	Head stays still until trailing shoulder forces it up		Raising head too soon or too late

PUTTING

Skill	Cue	Alternate Cue	Common Error
Stance	Feet and club, like a fence post perpendicular (90°) to hole or target line	Target line	Club slanted, no target line
Head Position	Top of head against a wall	Head still	Top of head points to sky
Focus of Eyes	Eyes over ball	Look at grass after hitting ball	Eyes not over ball
Straight Putt or Target Line	Make an imaginary line to hole or target line with eyes	Follow through toward hole or target line	Stopping the putter at impact, jabbing at the putt

PUTTING			
Skill	**Cue**	**Alternate Cue**	**Common Error**
Arm Swing (Figure 13.4)	Pendulum swing Short backswing, follow-through toward hole or target line	Swing from shoulders Stroke through ball and don't stop	Too much wrist action No follow-through, jabbing at putt at contact
Blade of Putter	Keep blade square to hole or target line throughout swing Slight forward hand press	Keep putter blade low to ground Hand press makes a more consistent roll of ball	Putter head lifts off ground Putter straight up and down
Mental Imagery	Imagine the ball going into the cup	Wait to hear ball go into cup	Looking up to see if ball goes into cup

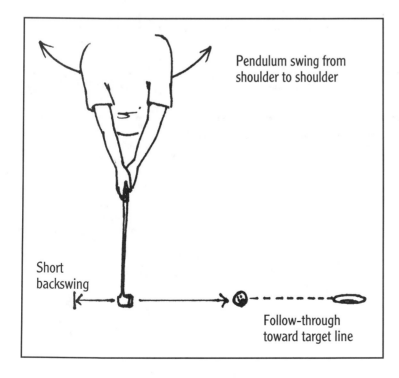

Pendulum swing from shoulder to shoulder

Short backswing

Follow-through toward target line

FIGURE 13.4 Arm Swing for Putting.

CHIPPING

Skill	Cue	Common Error
Stance	Play ball off back foot Choke up on the club Sit on bar stool Bend knees slightly	Playing ball off front foot or middle stance Standing up straight with legs straight
Wrists	Keep wrists firm	Letting wrists break at contact
Arms	Keep right elbow close to hip	Keeping elbow away from hip
Swing	Use a short backswing with a good, full follow-through	Taking a full backswing; no follow-through
Right Knee	Initiate swing with right knee	Keeping right knee away from hole; right knee does not face hole
Follow-Through	Follow-through toward hole, like tossing a ball to hole	Stopping at contact with ball

SAND SHOT

Skill	Cue	Common Error
Stance (Figure 13.5)	Be careful not to ground club	Placing club face in sand
Feet	Dig feet into the sand; open face at address	Failing to dig feet into sand, closed face
Swing	Swing fully	Digging into sand

Dig feet into sand

Use high follow-through

Head stays still until
trailing shoulder
forces it up

Take sand
with you

FIGURE 13.5 Sand Shot.

SAND SHOT		
Skill	**Cue**	**Common Error**
Eyes/Hands	Look at the sand 2 to 3 inches behind ball during entire swing	Looking at ball
	Head stays still until trailing shoulder forces it up	Raising head too soon or too late
Follow-Through	Make sure to follow-through toward the hole; take the sand with you	Digging club in sand; closed face
	Use a high follow-through	Stopping; no follow-through
Light Sand	Use a soft full swing	Using a hard swing
Heavy Sand	Use a hard full swing	Using a soft swing

WIND SHOT		
Skill	**Cue**	**Common Error**
Wind in Front of Golfer	Play ball off back foot for a low shot	Playing ball off front foot or middle of stance
	Decrease club number; for example, change 5 iron to 3 iron	Using a club number that is too high
Wind Behind Golfer	Play ball off front foot	Playing ball off back foot or middle of stance
	Increase club number; for example, change 5 iron to 7 iron	Using a club number that is too low

HILL SHOTS			
Skill	**Cue**	**Alternate Cue**	**Common Error**
Golf Ball Lies Downhill (Figure 13.6)	Play ball off high foot Play ball off back foot		Playing ball in a straddle stance or off front foot
	Keep shoulders parallel to the grass like airplane wings	Keep spine perpendicular to hill	Leaning forward
Beginner	Aim to the left; ball will go right		Aiming straight
Intermediate	Wrists break earlier to close club face		
Golf Ball Lies Uphill	Play ball off high foot Play ball off front foot		Playing ball in a straddle stance or off back foot
	Keep shoulders parallel to the grass like airplane wings	Keep spine perpendicular to hill	Leaning forward
Beginner	Aim to the right; ball will go left		Aiming straight
Intermediate	Wrists break later to keep club face open longer		

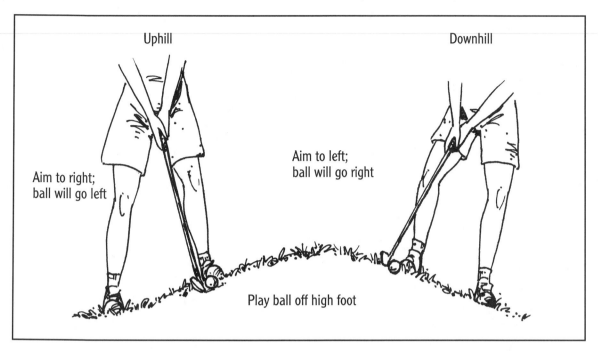

FIGURE 13.6 Hill Shots.

LOW BALLS		
Skill	**Cue**	**Common Error**
Feet	Play ball off back foot	Playing ball in a straddle stance or off front foot
Club Face	Square the club face	Open or very closed club face
Swing	Normal swing	No follow-through

Chapter 14

Pickle-Ball

INTRODUCTION

Many people ask the question: "What is Pickle-Ball?" Pickle-Ball is a paddle game that is a combination of tennis, badminton, and Ping-Pong. The game is played on a doubles badminton court (20 × 44 feet) using a perforated plastic ball and wooden paddles. The doubles badminton court on the gymnasium floor can be converted to a Pickle-Ball court simply by attaching the nets to the volleyball/badminton net standards at a height of 3 feet. Pickle-Ball can also be played on the inside singles lines on the tennis court. Pickle-Ball is an ideal lead-up game for teaching tennis and racquet skills.

The strategies of the game include lobbing, overhead slamming, passing drive shots from the baseline, and fast volley exchanges at the net. The game is played by four people; a fifth person can be designated to be the scorekeeper, which helps accommodate large PE classes and provides the opportunity for that student to learn the official rules of the game. Many teachers have emphasized how Pickle-Ball has been effective in developing the students' reflexes and eye-hand coordination skills along with quickness and agility. Pickle-Ball is a success-oriented game because after the player strikes the ball, the perforations slow the ball down in midflight, thereby promoting longer rallies and providing an equalizing factor for differences in strength, skill, and athletic ability. Many teachers are adding Pickle-Ball to their curricula because students can become successful with the game the first time they try it.

Pickle-Ball is played mainly during the fall and winter months and is a good unit to present before tennis because many of the teaching cues are similar. For example, two cues used for the forehand stroke for tennis and Pickle-Ball are "Hold your arm in a cast" and "Finish on edge." The only major adjustment would be the longer racquet. We have found that students who become successful with the game of Pickle-Ball are not as intimidated when learning the game of tennis. Another way to introduce Pickle-Ball is to start with a tennis unit, then add Pickle-Ball, and finish with a tennis unit.

SKILLS LISTED WITH CUES

The cues for Pickle-Ball skills include the ready position, forehand and backhand swing (grip, stance, and stroke), lob and drive serves, volley and drop shots, topspin, backspin, and the overhead smash. Also provided are cues for singles and doubles boundaries and scoring, along with singles and doubles strategies.

TIP

1. A Pickle-Ball unit can be presented before or after a tennis unit, or on rainy days during a tennis unit. One need not cancel a tennis class at any level because of inclement weather if one has a gym (Figure 14.1).

EQUIPMENT TIPS

1. Tennis courts, badminton courts, volleyball courts, playgrounds, walls with white lines.
2. Wiffle balls of all sizes, softball-size Wiffle balls for beginners.
3. Solid wood paddles. The ball contacting the wood paddle has a tendency to stay on the paddle longer, giving the player the advantage with direct shots on the court. Plastic on plastic tends to spray all over the place and will not stay on the service of the racquet as long. Players have a harder time controlling the shots, and fewer rallies occur. Longer rallies are the result of good equipment.
4. The length of the paddle makes a difference in performance because it is light in weight and short. Players can feel more control with the racquet especially with backhand shots.

FIGURE 14.1   Substitute Pickle-Ball for Tennis on a Rainy Day.

TEACHING IDEAS

1. For large beginning classes have players hit the ball against the wall 10 times. This exercise gives them practice hitting forehands, backhands, and the like by themselves. They progress to the net when they can hit 10 in a row.
2. Use the modified two-bounce-limit rule for beginning classes or less fit players.
3. Have players feed the ball to each other using half court. This method encourages practicing technique and provides numerous practice trials.
   - Forehand and backhand baseline shot drill provides forehand and backhand stroke practice. This drill is practiced at the baseline.
   - Dink volley game: players stand behind nonvolley zone and hit drives back and forth like volley drills in tennis.
   - Hit offensive and defensive lob shots with a partner.
   - Overhead smash drill with a partner.
4. Volley the ball in the air with a partner. Your goal is to see how many times you can hit the ball back and forth keeping the ball in the air. This drill is good for eye-hand coordination.
5. Score on every serve. The side-out rule can be modified so that a point is scored on every serve. One player serves for a total of 5 serves, then the opponent serves for 5 serves until one player scores 10 points. If time permits, one player serves 10 serves, then the opponent serves 10 serves until one player scores 11 points. Different numbers of serves can be substituted.
6. Provide challenge drills, modified games, games or tournaments set up before class. These "early bird specials" encourage the students to come early (Strand, Reeder, Scantling, & Johnson, 1995).

FYI

For further information and special help, consult the following organization and source:

Douglas Smith, President
Pickle-Ball, Inc.
801 Northwest 48th Street
Seattle, WA 98107
Phone: (206) 784–4723
Fax: (206) 781–0782

Provides a free catalog on request. A rule book, 9-minute videotape for the game of Pickle-Ball, textbook, and equipment (paddles, balls, nets, standards, and sets) are also available at this address.

Curtis, J. (1985). *Pickleball for player and teacher*. Englewood, CO: Morton.

READY POSITION

Skill	Cue	Common Error
Stance	Knees bent	Knees locked
	Weight on balls of feet	Weight on heels
	Square to net	Not square with net
Move to Swing	Pivot and step for both forehand and backhand strokes	

FOREHAND STROKE

Skill	Cue	Common Error
Grip	Shake hands with racquet	Choking the paddle, holding too tight
	Form a V on top bevel	Extending first finger behind paddle head
Stance	Pivot and step	Legs not moving, body is parallel to net
Stroke	Arm in cast; firm wrists	Bending wrists or arm
	Brush crumbs off table	Scooping ball
	Wait for ball to drop	
	Hit ball in front of right hip	
	Finish with paddle on edge	Finishing with paddle flat

BACKHAND STROKE

Skill	Cue	Common Error
Grip	Form a V with $\frac{1}{4}$ clockwise turn	Failing to turn racquet
	Knuckle on top	
Stance	Pivot and step; get racquet back	Not taking racquet back soon enough

BACKHAND STROKE

Skill	Cue	Common Error
Stroke	Pull sword out of scabbard	
	Wait for ball to drop	
	Hit ball knee high	
	Finish with paddle on edge	Face of paddle tilted too far up or down

SERVING

Skill	Cue	Common Error
Lob (Figure 14.2)		
Foot Placement	One foot in front of baseline, other foot in back of baseline	Both feet behind baseline
Toss	Drop the ball then swing the paddle	Throwing ball up or not dropping ball
Swing	Like pitching horseshoes	
	Follow-through straight up to hit face with biceps	Follow-through too low
	Finish like Statue of Liberty	

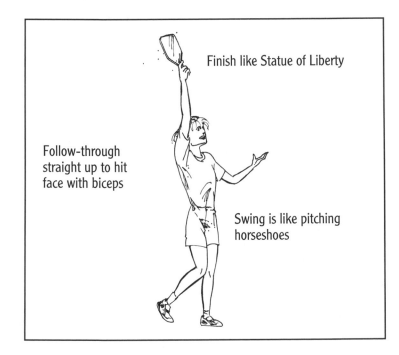

FIGURE 14.2 Lob Serve.

SERVING

Skill	Cue	Common Error
Drive (Figure 14.3)		
Foot Placement	One foot in front of baseline, other foot in back of baseline	Both feet behind baseline
Toss	Ball held waist high and out in front	Ball held too high or too low
	Paddle is held behind you, waist high	
	Wrist in cocked position	
Swing	Drop the ball then swing	Contacting the ball late
	Arm stiff, like a board, at contact	
Follow-Through	Paddle finishes on edge, shoulder level	

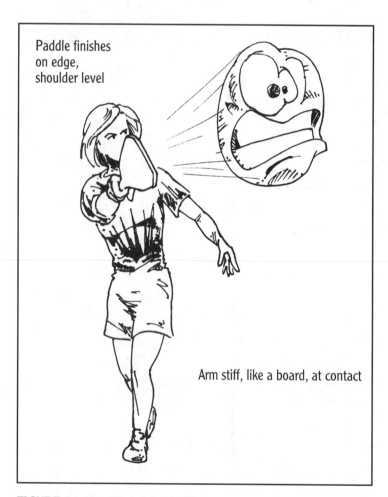

Paddle finishes on edge, shoulder level

Arm stiff, like a board, at contact

FIGURE 14.3 Drive Serve.

VOLLEY SHOT

Skill	Cue	Common Error
Ready Position	One foot behind nonvolley zone	Both feet in front of nonvolley zone (illegal)
	Paddle held at eye level	Paddle held too low
Legs and Swing Action	Step and punch	
	Little or no backswing	Too much backswing
	Slight turn of shoulders	Turning shoulders too much
	Meet ball in front of you	Letting ball come to you
	Keep racquet in peripheral vision	
Follow-Through	Contact ball in center of racquet	Contacting ball on racquet edge
	Punch the ball, play patty-cake	Swinging too hard
	Limit follow-through	Too long a follow-through
Strategy	Play just behind nonvolley zone	

DROP SHOT

Skill	Cue	Common Error
Swing	Graze shorts with racquet	Contact to side and front of body
	Slide racquet under ball	
	Love tap/soft touch	Hitting too hard
Contact	Open-face paddle to give ball underspin	Closing paddle face
	Push, lift, nudge, caress	
Follow-Through	Look in mirror at finish	Paddle is on edge
Strategy	Swing like a ground stroke when opponent is playing deep	Swinging like a drop shot

TOP AND BACK SPINS

Skill	Cue	Common Error
Top Spin	Swing racquet from low to high Like making a candy cane at end of swing	Swinging racquet level Finishing racquet on edge
Back Spin	Racquet swings high to low Shave the ball like shaving your face Cut flat under ball (see Figure 21.5)	Swinging racquet level Finishing racquet on edge

SMASH

Skill	Cue	Common Error
Position	Get in back of ball	Too far in front of ball
Contact with Ball	Contact ball in front of body Paddle face tilted toward floor	Contacting ball behind head Paddle face tilted toward wall
Follow-Through	Like a volleyball smash Recover quickly to ready position	No follow-through Off balance; can't recover to hit opponent's passing shot

SINGLES

Skill	Cue	Common Error
Boundaries	Tall skinny man (see Figure 3.4)	
Scoring	Can only score a point when serving (as in volleyball)	

SINGLES		
Skill	**Cue**	**Common Error**
Scoring *(cont.)*	When score is zero or even, serve in right court	
	When score is odd, serve in left court	
	Ball must bounce once in receiver's court as well as once in the server's court on the return: "bounce, bounce"	Volleying the ball before it has bounced once on each side of the net
	Play to 11, win by two points	
Strategies	Hit ball deep into opponent's court	Hitting ball in middle of court
	Hit most balls to opponent's weak side (usually backhand)	Hitting ball to player's forehand
	Hit ball to side to cause opponent to move	Hitting ball in middle of court
Server	Vary the serves—deep corners at opponents, hard, soft, etc.	
Receiver	Return ball to opponent's deep court	
Playing	Deep shots to sides	
	Weak sides when possible	
	Wait for errors, then attack net	
	Short volleys followed by deep lob to keep opponent off balance	
	Right at receiver	
	Mix up shots	Using same shot

DOUBLES		
Skill	**Cue**	**Common Error**
Boundaries	Short fat man (see Figure 3.4)	
Scoring	Server must have one foot behind baseline without touching the line	
	Serve across the net diagonally	
	Must clear nonvolley zone	
	Ball must bounce once in receiver's court as well as once in the server's court: "bounce, bounce"	
	First service: team A, one player serves	
	Second service: both players on team B serve, then both team A players serve	
	Server switches courts with teammate if point is scored by server	
	Service always starts in the right-hand court	
Strategies	To mix up drive and lob serves	Using same serve
	Accuracy is key over power	Trying to kill shots
Front/Back	Shadow your partner; attack the net	Not following your partner
Side to Side	Don't cross the property line; each one is responsible for ball in own side of court (see Figure 3.6)	Playing teammate's ball
	When ball goes close to middle line; call it	Not calling balls
	Communicate	

Racquetball

INTRODUCTION

Racquetball is a game of geometric angles that requires agility, speed, and accuracy. One of the great things about racquetball is never having to chase the ball. Racquetball allows one to practice shots and court movements by oneself.

Players should work on their forehand and backhand strokes first. Other strokes, such as the ceiling shot, can be developed from the successful use of these strokes.

When learning the forehand and backhand strokes, many players want to hit the ball hard and fast, but hitting too hard causes the player to lose control. Practicing technique and accuracy will help the player progress to the ultimate goal of hitting the ball harder and faster with better control.

Learning to track the ball is another skill players need to develop. A player must watch the angle of the ball coming off the wall to anticipate the next shot. Experience is the best teacher.

SKILLS LISTED WITH CUES

Included in this chapter are cues for the ready position, forehand and backhand strokes, drive and lob serves, corner and ceiling shots, and strategy of service return.

TIPS

1. Always wear proper, eye protection approved by the American Amateur Racquetball Association (AARA), no matter what your level of skill is. The ball can travel 80 to 100 miles an hour.
2. Adequately warm up and stretch before and after games.
3. If out of position or unsure, play defensively.
4. Concentrate on proper footwork (i.e., body parallel to sidewall for proper forehand).

EQUIPMENT TIPS

1. Use of proper racquet weight and string tension will prevent shoulder and arm pain.
2. Proper eye protection (AARA approved) is required.

3. Proper shoes provide ankle support and gripping.
4. Be sure racquet grip fits hand.

TEACHING IDEAS

1. Use the modified no-bounce-limit rule when starting with 5- to 7-year-olds. The player may allow the ball to bounce as many times as desired before hitting it.
2. Use the modified two-bounce-limit rule for 8- to 9-year-olds, junior racquetball leagues, beginning classes, or players who are not physically fit.
3. Stop and hit. Step, drop, and hit. Set up off front wall, step and hit. Continual rally, step and hit.
4. Play with scoring on each rally. Both server and receiver can score points.
5. One player tosses ball to rebound off wall; the other player hits the ball. This drill can be done with forehand and backhand strokes.

FYI

For further information and special help, consult the following organization and sources:

Jim Hiser
American Amateur Racquetball Association
1685 West Uintah
Colorado Springs, CO 80904–2921
Phone: (719) 635–5396
Fax: (719) 635–0685

Materials available:
1. Videos
2. Training materials
3. Racquetball magazine
4. Clothing

It's not always necessary to join a health club to play racquetball. Facilities are available for use at a nominal fee.

Edwards, L. (1988). *Racquetball*. Scottsdale, AZ: Gorsuch Scarisbrick.

Norton, C., & Bryant, J. E. (1986). *Beginning racquetball*. Englewood, CO: Morton.

READY POSITION AND GRIPS

Skill	Cue	Alternate Cue	Common Error
Ready Position	Knees bent		Standing upright
	Weight on inside of feet in order to push in either direction	Weight on inside of soles	Weight on heels
	Forearms on table		Arms (racquet) to side of body
Forehand Grip	V shape, top of bevel		Gripping too tightly
			Choking up on grip
	Index finger positioned to pull trigger	Squeeze trigger finger at impact	Incorrect placement of index finger
	Butt end of racquet in palm of hand (for more wrist action)		
Backhand Grip	Rotate V one bevel toward thumb	Turn clockwise	Failing to rotate grip from forehand to backhand

FOREHAND STROKE

Skill	Cue	Alternate Cue	Common Error
Hit Prep	Shoulders parallel to side wall	Set racquet first, then step, and then pivot	Hitting with body facing front wall
	Elbow above shoulder		Rushed and incomplete backswing
Execution (Figure 15.1)	Like skipping a rock		No wrist snap
	Shoulders dictate aim of ball	Shoulders parallel, hit parallel	Dropping front shoulder
			Lifting back shoulder
	Okay to contact ball at knee height; ankle, is best	Wait for ball to descend	Hitting ball at peak of bounce or ascent

Like skipping a rock

Pull left shoulder
through swing

Elbow extension,
snap wrist on contact

FIGURE 15.1 Forehand Execution.

FOREHAND STROKE			
Skill	**Cue**	**Alternate Cue**	**Common Error**
Execution *(cont.)*	Step into hit	Shift weight from back to front	Ball too high on front wall; racquet face tilted up
		Hit ball off front foot or close to front foot depending on shot	
	Watch ball hit strings		Watching target, not ball
	Elbow extension plus snap wrist on contact		Wrist in a cast
	Follow-through		No follow-through
Opposite Arm	Pull left shoulder through swing		Left arm hanging at side
	Hit and move to center of court		Standing still, not moving after shot

BACKHAND STROKE

Skill	Cue	Alternate Cue	Common Error
Hit Prep	Pivot—step—set racquet		
	Shoulders parallel to side wall		Shoulders perpendicular to side wall
	Elbow pointing to ground	Hitting elbow about 4 inches away from body	Elbow too close to body
	Wrist cocked		No wrist cock
Opposite Arm	Elbow pulling racquet back		Keeping left hand on racquet
Execution (Figure 15.2)	Shift weight back to front		No weight transfer
	Push belly button to front wall		No hip rotation

Racquet elbow pointing to ground

Okay to contact ball at knee height; ankle is best

Push belly button to front wall

FIGURE 15.2 Backhand Execution.

BACKHAND STROKE

Skill	Cue	Alternate Cue	Common Error
Execution (*cont.*)	Okay to contact ball at knee height; ankle is best	Wait for ball to descend	Hitting ball too high
	Snap wrist, like back-handing someone	Drive through with hitting shoulder	Arm in a cast
	Watch ball hit strings		Watching target or opponent not ball
	Hit ball off front foot		Hitting ball into floor; hitting off back foot
	Shoulder parallel to floor through swing	Shoulders dictate direction of ball	Swinging upward or dropping shoulder and skipping ball
	Follow-through at shoulder level	Racquet in "back-scratch position" (allows for more wrist snap in follow-through)	Open stance
	Hit and move to center of court		Hitting and standing still

SERVING

Skill	Cue	Alternate Cue	Common Error
Drive	Visualize bull's-eye on front wall 1 to 2 feet up		Not having a target
Ball Drop	Drop ball to allow extension and follow-through or consistent drop	Contact ball between calf and knee	
Bull's-eye	Should be $1/3$ of distance between ball drop and side wall—not more than 1 foot from ground	Drop—step—drive—move—follow ball	Hitting ball too high
	Hit and move toward center court		Inconsistent movement
			Not moving to center court after hitting

SERVING

Skill	Cue	Alternate Cue	Common Error
Drive (cont.) Bull's-eye (cont.)	Watch ball and know where opponent is		Not knowing where opponent is and not watching the ball
Lob	Firm wrist		Wrist snap
	Elbow extended		
	Like pitching horseshoes	Soft touch Like pushing ball instead of hitting ball	Hitting ball
	Contact ball between waist and shoulder		
	High follow-through	Pull arm to opposite shoulder	No follow-through
High	15 to 18 feet: graze side	Soft touch Contact on rise	Hitting ball too hard
Half	10 to 12 feet: approach opponent at shoulder height	Pull arm to opposite shoulder	No follow-through
	Hit and move to center of court; gain position		Not moving after serve

CORNER AND CEILING SHOTS

Skill	Cue	Alternate Cue	Common Error
Corner Shot	Pinch in corner	Low shot	Hitting too far from corner and too high
	Pinch—ball hits sidewall and then front wall, or vice versa		
	Near side corner		
	Eyes focus on target 1 to 2 feet from front		Eyes wandering
	Hit ball hard		Can't pinch ball if not hit hard enough

CORNER AND CEILING SHOTS

Skill	Cue	Alternate Cue	Common Error
Ceiling Shot	Forehand lob to ceiling Volleyball overhand server motion Aim to hit front lights depending on speed of ball		Hitting front wall first

SERVICE RETURN

Skill	Cue	Alternate Cue	Common Error
Strategy			
Beginner	Keep ball and self in center court	Consistency, try to read ball and play	No plan
Intermediate	Control rally with return of serve	Read serve and place ball to control rally	On the defense, not offense
Advanced	End rally with return of serve	Read serve and place ball to end rally	

Chapter 16

Skiing, Cross-Country

INTRODUCTION

Cross-country skiing through a countryside blanketed in snow can be enjoyed by young and old alike because it is relatively easy to master. We have designed the cues in this chapter to help students overcome their fear of being on skis for the first time and to help them perfect their skills.

SKILLS LISTED WITH CUES

The cues teach correct techniques of gripping and using poles, using bindings, falling, maintaining balance, striding, stopping, turning, skiing downhill, and climbing. These techniques bring a new dimension of freedom for students to explore and enjoy winter with its different terrains and moods.

    The sport of cross-country skiing involves vigorous aerobic exercise in frequently changing environmental conditions. Exposure to cold climate demands that cross-country skiers prepare for the worst weather conditions. To make cross-country skiing safer and more enjoyable, we have included safety and preparedness guidelines.

TIPS

1. Make sure you're taking a full pole plant, arm cycle, or pull cycle.
2. Some form of telemarketing, a skill used to go downhill on cross-country skis, needs to be learned. It can be used to slow you down or help you turn. Push the inside ski forward, let your outside knee drop to the front of the ski, and lean to the inside.

EQUIPMENT TIPS

Short Ski Trip

1. Hip pack including a water bottle.
2. Extra pair of gloves.
3. Light nylon windbreaker.

Long Ski Trip

Skiers venturing out for a longer tour that may last more than one hour and take them a considerable distance from a vehicle should carry additional equipment.

1. Larger pack with plenty of water, some snack food, hat, goggles.
2. Extra layer of insulation such as a wool sweater or pile jacket.
3. Extra pair of wool socks.
4. Spare ski tip.

Additional Items

5. Hot soup or hot drink.
6. Emergency space blanket to have something to sit on or to help warm someone.
7. Matches or a lighter.

Wooded and Unknown Areas

8. Compass and map are essential.
9. A range of waxes, a scraper, and a cork for waxable skis.

TEACHING IDEAS

1. One of the first skills to learn is to push and glide. Practice the glide. Push, then glide on opposite leg and count, "One–one thousand, two–one thousand, three–one thousand." Then push on the other side, glide with the opposite leg and count, "One–one thousand, two–one thousand, three–one thousand."
2. Another drill is to learn to pull, plant, and push with the opposite push leg.
3. Practice falling uphill; practice getting up. Lean into the hill to get up and put pressure on upper ski.
4. Practice on a golf course, a big open football field, a farmer's pasture, or some similar place before heading out to a cross-country trail. Become familiar with your skis, falling, and so on.
5. Practice breaking trail by keeping skis very close and in line.
6. Practice a progressive turn or smooth corner on the golf course, field, or pasture.
7. Find virgin snow or fresh deep powder, and practice breaking trail. A skier in fresh snow will have a slightly faster leg turnover.
8. Know the difficulty and distance of your trails before venturing out. Maps can be obtained at your local ski shops.

FYI

For further information and special help, consult the following organization:

Robyn Christiansen (head ski instructor)
PO Box 8007
Alta Ski School
Alta, UT 84092
Phone: (801) 742–2600

GRIPS—POLES—BINDINGS—FALLING

Skill	Cue	Alternate Cue	Common Error
Gripping Poles	Slide hand up into glove	Insert hand up through wrist strap	Inserting hand down through strap
	Grip both handle and strap	Pull against strap	Only gripping handle
	Allow handle to pivot against crease of thumb and index finger	Hand near top of handle	
	Light handshake with handle	Loose grip on handle	Tight grip on handle
Using Poles	Open hand to wave to people behind you	Loosen grip as hand extends behind you	Holding pole tightly through the stride
	Throw pole behind you with full-arm extension		Not releasing handle in extension
Traditional Three-Pin Bindings	Position skis level	Place perpendicular to fall line	Positioning skis on an incline
	Slide into slipper	Make a divot with toes	Not inserting toe of boot far enough
	Point toes toward ground and slide foot into binding		
Falling	Sit down in low chair on uphill side	Bend knees	Reaching out with arm to break fall
		Lean uphill	
	Fall to side	Fall onto legs and hips	Falling forward or backward

BALANCE

Skill	Cue	Alternate Cue	Common Error
Technique	Get in ready position	Assume landing position after a jump	Standing stiff
	Starting stance for a long-distance running race	Place skis shoulder-width apart	Skis too close
	Slight lean forward		
	Ski proud	Chest out, head up	Leaning too far back
	Look ahead		
	Knees are shock absorbers	Loose—bent knees	Hunching over
	Hands on side of steering wheel	Hands low, in front	Arms high and outside
	Keep weight evenly over both feet	Push into snow with feet	Weight on heels or balls of feet

FORWARD MOVEMENT

Skill	Cue	Alternate Cue	Common Error
Diagonal Stride	Most efficient technique for traveling forward		
	Exaggerated march step	Relaxed, fully extended walk	Stiff shuffle
			Looking at ski tips instead of looking ahead
			Not extending arms or legs at end of stride
	Ski proud	Chest out, head up	Hunching over
	Look ahead		Looking at ski tips
Double Poling (Figure 16.1)	Technique used for forward acceleration		
	Bow, like samurai warrior	Pull through handrails by bending forward	Not bending forward and throwing hands back

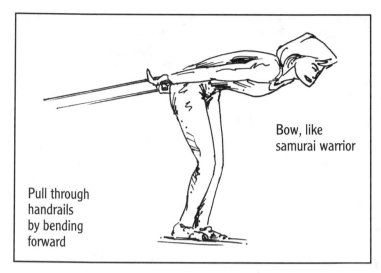

Pull through
handrails
by bending
forward

Bow, like
samurai warrior

FIGURE 16.1 Double Poling.

FORWARD MOVEMENT			
Skill	**Cue**	**Alternate Cue**	**Common Error**
Double Pole Stride	Fastest technique for forward travel, but not as efficient as the diagonal stride		
	Ride a scooter	Kick with one leg, glide with the other	Kicking leg; not springing hard enough off snow
	Ice-skating by pushing with only one leg	Weight shifts from one ski during the kick to both skis during glide	Not shifting weight between kick and glide
	Downhill skier pulling out of starting gate	Lean forward, plant both poles, then spring off ground	Not reaching far forward
	Reach far forward with poles		Stabbing at snow

SLOWING DOWN—TURNS—UPHILL MOVEMENT

Skill	Cue	Alternate Cue	Common Error
Snowplow	Technique for slowing down or stopping		
	Pigeon-toed squat	Make a wedge by driving inside edge into snow	Pushing with outside of heels
Skating Turns	Technique for making medium-large turns, preceded by the double-poling technique		
	Ice-skating turns with long exaggerated strides	Turn by stepping forward and to the side	Not transferring weight from feet
			Standing straight up
Herringbone (Figure 16.2)	Walk squatly like a duck	Make a wide V with toes pointing out	Making the V too narrow
		Dig inside edge of ski in	Skis flat on snow
	Ski proud	Keep torso upright	Bending and looking at ski tips

Walk squatly like a duck

Make a V-shape

Keep torso upright

Dig inside edge of ski in

FIGURE 16.2   Herringbone.

POWDER AND ICE SKIING			
Skill	**Cue**	**Alternate Cue**	**Common Error**
Powder	Traveling forward is more strenuous; turns may be more difficult because of snow on top of skis		
	Allow for more time to perform a turn, and plan on slower travel		
Icy Patches	Continue to travel straight across ice; avoid turning until in softer snow	Get into a balanced, stable position	Standing straight up
		Glide across ice	Leaning back

TOURING, RECREATIONAL, AND RACING POSTURES

Skill	Cue	Common Error
Postures (Figure 16.3)		
Touring	Body more erect	
Recreational	Project body farther forward (helps with glide)	Standing tall
Racing	Lean diagonally forward to propel aggressively	Standing tall

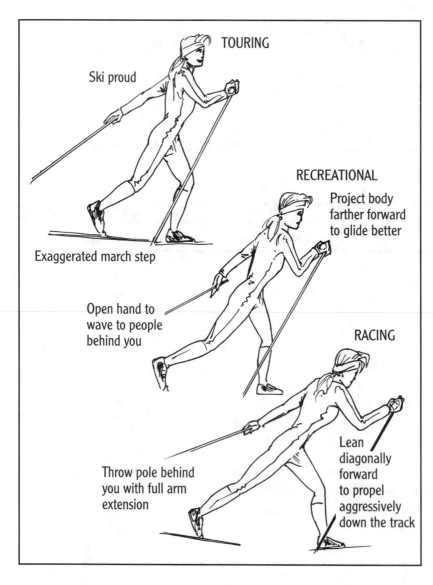

FIGURE 16.3 Variations of Posture.

Chapter 17

Soccer

INTRODUCTION

In the summer of 1994 one of the world's greatest sporting events was held in the United States, the World Cup for Soccer. Because of the multitude of nations participating, this tournament requires a two-and-a-half-year period for teams to qualify. After the qualifying period, the final 24 teams assemble in a designated country for a month-long tournament. Youth soccer is one of the fastest-growing sports in the country, and because of the success of the 1994 World Cup, it should experience an even larger increase in its membership.

As this increase takes place, there will be a greater demand at the junior high and high school levels for instruction. Therefore, physical education teachers will need to understand the basic skills and tactics of the game in order to provide their students with an enjoyable learning experience. When implemented correctly, soccer offers a good fitness base and healthy social climate.

The appealing features for adding soccer to the curriculum are that it's fun, it improves overall fitness, and it is relatively inexpensive because essential equipment need be no more than a ball, marking cones, and scrimmage vests.

SKILLS LISTED WITH CUES

In this chapter, the following cues are provided that will assist in teaching the skills and tactics necessary to play the game. For the field player, these skills include dribbling, control trap, chipping, passing, lofted aerial pass, volley, shooting, challenging (tackling), heading, and defensive and offensive tactics. For the goalie, these skills include punting, catching, diving, positioning, and distribution.

TIP

1. Warm-up should consist of approximately 8 to 10 minutes of moderate physical activity, such as jogging or a game of tag. This will ensure a proper increase in body core temperature prior to stretching.

EQUIPMENT TIPS

1. Soccer balls: synthetic leather balls, size 5, work well and are not expensive. Red kick balls should not be used for soccer. Less skilled players can use nerf soccer balls.
2. Shoes need to be comfortable, not too tight. Avoid knots in the laces.
3. Shin guards (if available).
4. Small baby cones can be used to outline the field, and large cones can be used for corners and goals.
5. Mini nets 3 feet high and 3 feet wide can be used for goals.
6. Cleats are not recommended for physical education classes but are advised for soccer teams.

TEACHING IDEAS

1. Finish sessions with small-sided games for middle school students and, if possible, full-field games for secondary students. Award 1 point for hitting inside large-cone goals and 2 points for hitting inside net.
2. Play modified games with four to seven players on each team. Let everyone have a turn at each position.
3. Introduce two balls in one game and two goalies. Play with two balls. For coed classes have a soccer ball of a specific color for the girls and a ball of another color for both boys and girls. Girls can play with both balls.
4. In coed games, boys can kick with left leg only.
5. Tournament: Four teams with 8, 9, or 10 players on each team; use half of a football field, 30 yards wide and 50 yards long.

FYI

For further information and special help, consult the following organizations:

American Youth Soccer Organization
5403 West 138th Street
Hawthorne, CA 90250
Phone: (310) 643–6455
Fax: (310) 643–5310

U.S. Soccer Federation
1801–1811 South Prairie Avenue
Chicago, IL 60616
Phone: (312) 808–1300
Fax: (312) 808–1301

DRIBBLING

Skill	Cue	Alternate Cue	Common Error
Technique	Caress ball in stride		Keeping ball too far in front allowing it to escape
	Player can use inside, outside, sole, or laces of shoes	Contact made on various areas of foot, depending on situational demands	Poor recognition of situation resulting in improper contact and loss of possession
	Close control, pushing firmly	Head up	Head always down
	Change pace and direction	Arms out with elbows bent for balance	Pace too hard or too soft

TRAPPING

Skill	Cue	Alternate Cue	Common Error
Control Trap (Figure 17.1)	Catching an egg	Water balloon catch	Meeting with too hard a surface
	Present controlling surface to ball: example, foot or thigh is raised up toward ball and pulled back on contact	Square up with ball and cushion on contact	Ball bounces too far to be controlled
		Cushion on contact	No cushion on contact

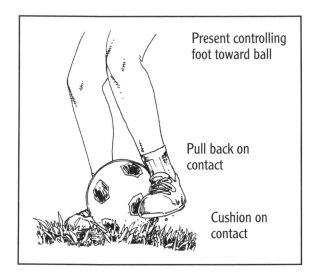

Present controlling foot toward ball

Pull back on contact

Cushion on contact

FIGURE 17.1 Control Trap.

CHIPPING

Skill	Cue	Alternate Cue	Common Error
Technique	Popping a billiard ball with a pool stick		Striking too high on ball will not provide backspin
	Straight-on approach	Square up with ball	Stabbing too soft under ball does not allow it to rise
	Quick hard stab under ball	Keep head steady	
	Very little follow-through creates backspin	Strike where ball contacts ground	Too much follow-through will cause ball to be propelled too low

PASSING

Skill	Cue	Alternate Cue	Common Error
Push Pass on the Ground	Pendulum swing with foot		Improper momentum causes pace to be too soft or hard and inaccurate
	Inside-of-foot contact	Follow-through in front of body	Follow-through goes across body
	Ankle firm	Flex knee and strike through midline of ball	Ankle loose, not allowing player to guide ball
	Nonkicking foot alongside ball	Flex nonkicking foot balancing leg	Nonkicking foot points away from target causing poor follow-through
	Knee of kicking leg over ball on contact	Correct weight of pass	Knee of kicking leg too far behind ball may cause ball to rise

PASSING			
Skill	**Cue**	**Alternate Cue**	**Common Error**
Lofted Aerial Pass of 15 Yards or More	Wide approach with nonkicking foot; use surface between laces and inside of foot	Toes pointed down, foot turned slightly out	Nonkicking foot too close to ball causing it to strike too high on ball
	Strike ball where ball touches grass, with good follow-through	Keep ankle locked when striking	Ankle loose, causing ball to go astray
	Nonkicking foot plants to side and slightly behind ball	Follow-through in front of body	Nonkicking foot too close to ball, keeping ball low
	Lean back		Body too erect, not allowing ball to rise

VOLLEY			
Skill	**Cue**	**Alternate Cue**	**Common Error**
Technique	Contact made through vertical midline, follow-through from center of ball to top as if ball is rolling off foot causing topspin		Contact is made underneath ball making it rise
	Nonkicking foot alongside as in push pass	On contact, knee slightly over ball	Nonkicking foot too far behind ball
	Ankle firm, toes pointed down	Square up with ball and use full instep when striking	Toes pointing up causing ball to go straight up
	Land on kicking foot	Head steady, constantly watching ball	Head not steady on contact, causing ball to go astray

SHOOTING (INSTEP DRIVE)

Skill	Cue	Alternate Cue	Common Error
Technique	Firing a cannonball		Leg not properly pulled back, resulting in less momentum through ball
	Pull back kicking leg	Load up kicking leg	Follow-through across body carries ball wide of target
	Nonkicking foot alongside ball pointing at target	After follow-through land on kicking foot	Body leaning back causes ball to rise
	Ankle firm, toes pointing down	Head down and steady with weight over ball to keep ball low	Ankle loose, head not steady, causing ball to stray

CHALLENGING (TACKLING)

Skill	Cue	Alternate Cue	Common Error
Definition	Meet ball at same time as opponent		Went fishing and caught nothing (player not focused on ball)
Technique	Tackling foot turned out at right angle	Weight behind ball	Diving in or poor timing
	Swing through as in push pass	On contact, weight of body goes through ball	Tentative challenge with kicking leg or going in too strong and out of control (can result in broken leg)
	Powerful controlled follow-through	Balance with arms out	

HEADING			
Skill	**Cue**	**Alternate Cue**	**Common Error**
Heading (Figure 17.2)	Bend at the waist		Bumping ball and leaning back, causing improper follow-through
	Meet ball with forehead	Project ball out and away from body	Making contact with ball too high on head (headache)
	Eyes open; watch ball onto forehead	Lean back, tighten stomach muscles, and propel torso and head forward when contacting the ball	Closing eyes
	Weight of body goes through ball		Striking too low on ball causes ball to spin upward; striking too high on ball may cause ball to hit nose

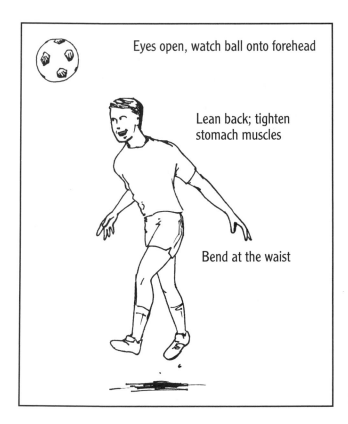

Eyes open, watch ball onto forehead

Lean back; tighten stomach muscles

Bend at the waist

FIGURE 17.2   Heading.

PUNTING

Skill	Cue	Alternate Cue	Common Error
Technique (Figure 17.3)			
Hand Position	Like holding a skunk	Hold ball out away	Holding ball too close to chest
Drop Action	Drop the ball		
Kicking Leg	Like an underhand serve in volleyball	Shoelaces flat	
	Like kicking a football	Pull back kicking leg	Swinging leg from standing position does not create momentum
	Swing leg under body making contact with ball below knee		
Support Leg	Support leg plants simultaneously with dropping of ball		Ball is met too high on leg with shins or too low on end of toes

Like holding a skunk

Drop the ball

Pull back kicking leg

FIGURE 17.3 Punt.

GOALTENDING

Skill	Cue	Alternate Cue	Common Error
Catching	Making a W with thumbs and index fingers	Keep thumbs and heel of hand behind ball for solid support	Keeping hands to side of ball, allowing ball to slip through
	Elbows bent	Fingers spread	Arms held too rigid, not allowing for controlled comfort when receiving
	Cushion on contact while pulling ball back in front of body	Soft hands	Ball meets hard surface and bounces away
Punching	Clear ball out when unable to grab safely	High and wide	Punching ball down toward feet of offensive players
	Fists clenched and together	Elbows cocked ready to release when contacting ball	Extending arms, not allowing for punching action
	Time jump	Meet ball as high as possible and under control when striking	Meeting ball too low because of poor timing
Receiving	Knee and foot together		Knee and foot not close enough to each other, leaving space for ball to go through
Low Balls (Figure 17.4)	Scoop shovel	Cup hands together and create a shovel	Hands spread apart, allowing ball to squeak through
	Elbows bent and slightly tucked in toward body	Watch ball into arms	Arms too stiff, not allowing to receive comfortably
	Bring into chest	Always secure ball in safe area in front of body	Collecting ball to side, not providing second surface in case ball is mishandled

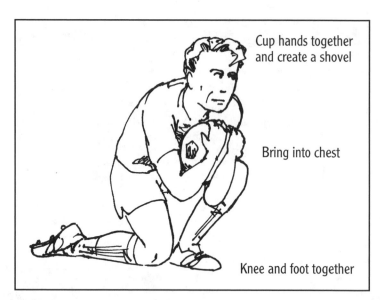

Cup hands together and create a shovel

Bring into chest

Knee and foot together

FIGURE 17.4   Goalie Receiving Low Balls.

GOALTENDING

Skill	Cue	Alternate Cue	Common Error

Receiving *(cont.)*
High Balls
(Figure 17.5)
	Meet at highest
	   comfortable point
	Pull ball in
		Hands technique same
		   as in catching cues
		Reach out with both
		   hands
			Meeting ball too low,
			   allowing opposing
			   players the chance
			   to make contact

Lobbing **(20+ Yards)**	Cup ball in hand and forearm		Ball not securely held

	Throw a javelin	Rotation begins from
		   behind body and
		   level with hip
			Trajectory is limited
			   by poor rotation

	Release overhead and
	   in front of body
		Arms swing from hip
		   behind body, and then
		   overhead
			Releasing ball too low,
			   limiting distance of lob

Pull ball in

Reach out with both hands

Meet at highest
comfortable point

FIGURE 17.5 Goalie Receiving High Balls.

GOALTENDING			
Skill	**Cue**	**Alternate Cue**	**Common Error**
Throwing (10–20+ Yards)	Throwing a baseball	Grasp ball with one hand and cock arm	Arm not properly pulled back does not allow for quick release
	Shove ball forward	Throwing action comes from side of head next to ear	Release of ball is too slow; ball may be intercepted
	Twisting action will limit bounce for player receiving	Hard push from side of head	No spin on release makes ball bounce and difficult to receive
Rolling (≤ 10 Yards)	Rolling a bowling ball	Cup ball into hand and forearm as in lob	Holding ball too loose
	Underhand pitch in softball	Swing from behind body and past hip	Too short a follow-through will not allow ball to reach target
	Roll in front of or directly to player's feet	Keep ball low with no bounce	Releasing ball too high causes it to bounce and be hard to control

DEFENSE		
Skill	**Cue**	**Common Error**
Tactics	Funnel players in front of goal	Team is spread out in front of goal, creating space for attackers to exploit
	Players in front of goal will be close together, closing down goal-scoring options for attackers	Defense posture is loose, allowing goal-scoring opportunities
	*Create lines of defense for depth and support	Players are caught in a straight line across the field, allowing for penetration with a single pass
	*Delay opposition as far away from goal as possible to allow players to recover	Team in possession allowed to freely advance forward
	†Players closest to ball must provide immediate pressure	Closest individual defender does not delay attacker
	†Keep playing space narrow for opponents by channeling toward touchline or supporting defenders	Defending with body square to attacker allows for options to the sides or through legs
	†Keep balance of team organized through communication	Confusion and disarray in defense through lack of communication
	If ball cannot be won directly from challenge, clear ball away from danger area either upfield or over touchline	Players in their defensive third of the field attempt to advance ball under extreme pressure and lose possession, possibly creating goal-scoring opportunity for opponent
	*Once ball has been recovered offense begins immediately	Slow transition from defending to attacking
	Results can be achieved through man-to-man marking, zonal marking, or a combination	

*Important when the defense brings the ball up; supports the offensive attack.
†Important in an attacking situation on defense.

OFFENSE		
Skill	**Cue**	**Common Error**
Tactics	*Offense begins immediately when ball has been won	Delay in transition may result in loss of possession
	*All players are involved in offense from point of recovery	Player fails to move into offense, limiting options
	*Create options by utilizing width of field	Attacking players squeezing in toward center of field closes down space for players in possession
	†Quickly move ball into defensive half through quick, short, crisp passes to open players or directly to forward target	Delay in advancing ball allows defense to recover
	†Forward movement of offensive players not in possession creates dribbling or passing opportunities for player with ball	Lack of movement provides few options for player with ball
	Vary focus and method of attack	Team becomes predictable and easy to defend
	Creativity and imagination in final offensive third of field is vital to creating chances for scoring	Lack of imagination and creativity stifles attack
	†Taking risk in front of opponents' goal is encouraged as loss of possession does not create immediate danger	Without taking risk in front of defensive team's goal, scoring will become difficult
	The ultimate objective in soccer is to score goals; therefore, always attempt to end attack with a shot or goal	Teams that play not to lose rather than to win develop players who find the game to be dull and boring

*Important when offense begins an attack.
†Important when offense is attacking and trying to score.

Chapter 18

Softball, Fast-Pitch

INTRODUCTION

"Safe!" yells the umpire, as the runner slides into home. The crowd goes wild as the home team wins the tournament.

One of fast-pitch softball's unique features is that it is a hometown game that pulls a community together. Recreation departments accommodate people of different ages and provide opportunities for them to join youth, coed, female, and male leagues.

Nearly every town, small or large, has a ball diamond where residents gather to enjoy the cool evenings and chat with neighbors while watching the game.

Opportunities to teach fast-pitch skills can begin in the middle school and continue though high school and college.

SKILLS LISTED WITH CUES

Softball requires a variety of skills: throwing, catching, windmill pitching, batting, sacrifice bunting, baserunning, runner-on-base techniques, fielding fly balls and ground balls, catching pitches, fielding, and sliding (straight-in slide). The use of these organized cues and progressions can be very beneficial.

TIPS

1. Going over players' positions before the season begins creates harmony and team success. Explain the mental and physical expectations of each player and her or his role on the team. For example, a player's responsibility might be sitting on the bench, warming up ready to hit or run, or perhaps to play second or third base if an infielder is injured or is not having a good game. A team member who plays second base in one game may play shortstop or be a defensive replacement in the next game. This approach develops a team concept. If a player makes an error, have the person focus on the next play. Direct the energy into a positive focus. Pick up a rock, pretend the rock is the error, and toss it—get rid of it.
2. Make practice fun and competitive! At the beginning of practice have a verbal cue, for example, "blue." When they hear the cue "blue," the players stop and do what the coach explained they would do at beginning of practice. The coach can have a variety of motivational ideas or conditioning exercises to give to the players. For exam-

ple, perform 5 sprints, 10 sit-ups, 15 push-ups, or some other exercise; give a high five to a player standing next to you; run together and laugh; tell a player something positive; or call a player's name, and have that player tell the team what they are going to do. At completion continue practice where the coach left off. Change off with hitting one day and defense the next day.

3. Use of batting tees provides instant feedback and helps correct batting errors more quickly. Pitching machines build confidence in batting.

EQUIPMENT TIPS

1. Glove: Outfielder's glove is longer for more range; infielder's glove is shorter for more quickness. Use a batting glove under the glove to help pad it.
2. Batting gloves also can be used to protect the hand when diving back to base or sliding into base.
3. Boys, girls, women, and men should use a bat light enough to control and swing for quickness. Start with a 22-ounce bat for young girls and boys and go up to a 25- to 28-ounce bat for college-age athletes.
4. Sliding shorts, knee and elbow pads, and sweat bands are especially good for sliding drills to avoid scratches and abrasions.
5. Steel cleats add quickness and agility for defense, running base paths, and preparation for sliding.

TEACHING IDEAS

1. Warm up arm: First throw short distances (emphasize correct throwing technique); then move to longer distances.
   a. Short-hop drill: Have a partner throw ball at receiver's feet or glove when in a defensive position, so the player can't catch it in the air.
   b. Short underhand or overhand lob drill: Correct technique, close and long pop-ups; 10 short hops: always catch with two hands; 10 pop-ups: call pop-ups, move feet, communicate "mine," move with glove tucked.
2. Quick-hands partners drill: Catch the ball with two hands, rotate the glove to see the ball, grip it, and get rid of it as quickly as possible. The goal is to see who can get rid of the ball the fastest.
3. Soft-toss drill against a fence: Partner stands on bench or chair and drops ball straight down. Hitter works on quick hands, and ball contact.
4. Bingo drill: Place a batting tee and ball at home plate; place another batting tee and ball directly in front of the first tee. The batter's goal is to hit the first ball off the tee into the other ball straight in front of it. Yell "Bingo" if the goal is accomplished. This drill helps timing, batting stride, quick hands, and knowing where the batter should be contacting the ball.
5. Throw ball to fielders, progress to side/side, up and back, hitting ball with bat.
6. Lateral drill: All players line up at third base position; coach hits ball to first player in line. That player fields the ball, then throws home; moves to the shortstop position and fields ball, throws home; moves to second base position, fields ball and throws home; moves to first base position, fields ball, throws home. That player stops at first base and waits until last fielder goes. The fielders in line repeat the same drill. Everyone goes back around. All players in line encourage the fielder who is up.
7. Baserunning and defensive strategy drills are best taught without batting to permit more offensive and defensive plays (repetitions).
8. Give players opportunities to play all positions.

```
┌─────────────────────────────────────────────────────────────┐
│                           FYI                                 │
├───────────────────────────────────────────────────────────────┤
```

For further information and special help, consult the following organizations:

Fast Pitch World
PO Box 1190
St. Charles, IL 60174
Phone: 1–800–591–1222

1. Updated equipment, notebooks, techniques, rules, and umpire information.
2. Video: 12 fast-pitch USA videos.
3. *Fast Pitch World Magazine*.

National Softball Coaches Association (NSCA)
409 Vandiver Drive Suites
Columbia, MO 65202
Phone: (314) 875–3033
Fax: (314) 875–2924

All junior high, high school, and college coaches are welcome to become members.

THROWING

Skill	Cue	Alternate Cue	Common Error
Grip	Hold ball in pads of two fingers		Gripping the ball in palm
Stance	Stand sideways	Point glove-hand shoulder at target	Standing forward
Throwing Action (Figure 18.1)	Take a long step toward target		Not stepping, stepping too high, stepping across the body
	Take arm straight down and stretch it way back	Make an L with throwing arm	Bringing ball behind head
	Wrist snap		Keeping weight on back foot
Focus	Both eyes focus on target		Looking anywhere else

Stretch arm way back to make an L

Stand sideways

Take a long step toward target

FIGURE 18.1   Throwing the Ball.

CATCHING		
Skill	**Cue**	**Common Error**
Hand Action	Reach out with hands, pull ball in	Hands too close to body
	Give with ball	Not pulling ball in
	Squeezing ball	Spreading fingers
Focus of Eyes	Watch ball go into glove or fingers	Taking eyes off ball; not tracking the ball

WINDMILL PITCH

Skill	Cue	Alternate Cue	Common Error
Stance	Square to target Keep front heel and back toe on rubber		Perpendicular to target No contact with rubber
Grip	Three-finger grip (thumb and three fingers) Keep ball in glove or hand, waist high	Hold ball in fingers, without palm touching ball	Holding ball in palm of hand Ball too high or too low Ball not in glove
Arm Swing (Figure 18.2)	Raise hand above head Back-circle to release point		Bringing arm to side

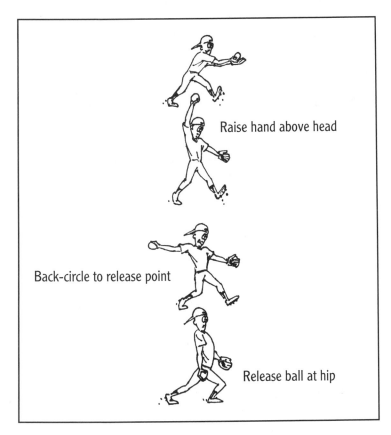

Raise hand above head

Back-circle to release point

Release ball at hip

FIGURE 18.2 Arm Swing for Windmill Pitch.

WINDMILL PITCH

Skill	Cue	Alternate Cue	Common Error
Release (Figure 18.3)	Release ball at hip		Releasing in front or behind hip
	Turn belt buckle to target	Make sure to rotate hips	Letting arrm do all the work
	Snap wrist on release	Keep wrist relaxed	Keeping wrist stiff
	Follow-through after wrist snap		Bending elbow as hand finishes up by head
	Point toe at catcher	Push off rubber with back foot	Not striding directly at plate

Turn belt buckle to target

Snap wrist on release

Push off rubber with back foot

FIGURE 18.3 Release for Windmill Pitch.

HITTING		
Skill	**Cue**	**Common Error**
Stance	Stand sideways	Standing forward
	Feet slightly wider apart than-shoulder-width	Feet too far apart or too close together
	Weight over balls of feet	Weight on heels
	Heels lightly touching	
	More weight on back leg	
Arm Swing	Hitter should think "shoulder to shoulder" (start swing with chin on front shoulder; finish swing with chin on back shoulder)	Moving head during the swing Head too tense
Hip Rotation	Snap or rotate back hip at pitcher, drive body through ball, take photograph of pitcher with belly button	Not rotating hip
	Throw hands through softball: "Slow feet, quick hands"	Using arms instead of wrists
Focus of Eyes	Imagine middle of softball has a face and is laughing at you; try to hit the ball in the face	Not seeing ball hit bat
	Watch ball all the way into catcher's mitt	
Step	Step 3 to 6 inches (stride should be more of a glide)	Overstriding causes bat to drop during swing (jarring step)
	"Step to hit"	Hitter "steps and then hits"
Follow-Through	Top hand rolls over bottom hand; bat goes all around the body	
Teaching Progression	Teach cues in order given (first three); then add others as needed	
	Take your right palm to the pitcher; draw a straight line through your chest with left thumb	

HITTING FOR INEXPERIENCED BATTERS

Skill	Cue	Common Error
Checkpoints for Coaches	If the batter is not gripping, standing, or holding bat correctly, coach could correct the player individually	Don't use these cues unless a player needs assistance; give one at a time.
Grip	Hold bat in base of fingers (this technique allows wrist to roll freely and generates bat speed) Align knuckles	Holding bat in palm of hand; squeezing bat
Closed Stance	Place feet shoulder-width apart, then move front foot toward plate (helps untrained hitter step toward pitcher)	Stepping back
Bat Position	Bat held armpit high and far enough away from the body that two of the player's fists could fit Back elbow held away from body	Holding bat too close to shoulder Dropping back elbow
Bat Angle	Straight up in air or up and angled slightly over back shoulder	Cradling bat around head; bat pointing back toward pitcher

SACRIFICE BUNT

Skill	Cue	Alternate Cue	Common Error
Grip	Grip bat lightly with thumb and two fingers		
Action	Pivot toward pitcher, square body to pitcher		Keeping side toward pitcher
	Bend knees		Legs straight
	Slide top hand up to trademark, keep bat level		Choking too high on bat with top hand, keeping fingers on back side
			Not keeping bat level
	Place bat in front of plate at top of strike zone		Keeping bat behind body
Contact	Play catch with ball	Give with the ball	Dropping bat to ball
			Swinging at a ball
			Going for a pitch out of strike zone

BASERUNNING

Skill	Cue	Alternate Cue	Common Error
Running to First	Push off with back leg		Swinging arms wildly
	Run through base		Pointing toes out
	Dig dig dig	Full acceleration	Shortening or lengthening stride
	Run with form	Hammer nails	Leaping at base
Extra Base	Make loop at base		Looking at base
	Hit inside of base		Hitting outside of base
	Round bag and jog back if necessary		Looping too wide

RUNNER ON BASE

Skill	Cue	Common Error
Ready Position	Square body to next base	Keeping body perpendicular
	Take stagger start	Keeping feet together
	Keep right foot a stride behind base	
	Push off left foot, stride with right	
Break	Start stride at top of pitcher's windup	Leaving before pitch is released
	Push off at release	
	Rock 'n' go	
Approach	Pump arms with stride	
	Hammer in nails	
	Round base and look for coach	

FIELDING FLY BALLS			
Skill	**Cue**	**Alternate Cue**	**Common Error**
Glove	Out in front of body		Palm up or glove to side
	Raise glove toward ball		Glove down
Body	Square to ball		Side to ball
	Point fingers upward, thumbs together	Fingers toward sky; thumbs touch	Fingers down; hands apart
	Stay behind ball, block out sun		Not getting behind ball
Action	Soft glove		
	Give with catch		Arms stiff
	Cover ball with throwing hand	Catch ball with two hands	Catching with one hand
Focus	See ball into glove		Looking away too soon in haste to make the throw

FIELDING GROUND BALLS			
Skill	**Cue**	**Alternate Cue**	**Common Error**
Glove (Figure 18.4)	Put fingers of glove in dirt		Glove too high
	Keep palms up, pinkies together	Pinkies touch, fingers point toward dirt	Hands apart; fingers pointing toward sky
	Keep glove in front of body		Glove off to side of body
Body	Keep body square to ball		Body too high off the ground and stiff, not willing to give
	Keep butt down	Like sitting on a stool	Standing tall
	Stay behind ball		
	Keep knees flexed		

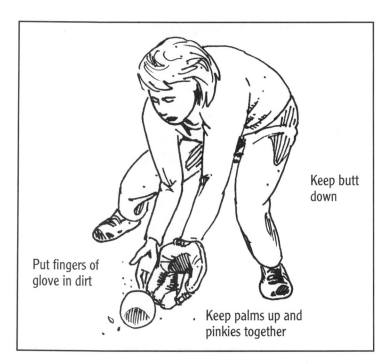

Keep butt down

Put fingers of glove in dirt

Keep palms up and pinkies together

FIGURE 18.4   Fielding a Ground Ball.

THE CATCHER		
Skill	**Cue**	**Common Error**
Stance	Crouch over balls of feet	Body held erect with weight over heels or down on knees
	Align right toe with left heel, toes out	
	Keep weight over balls of feet	
	Keep knees flexed, butt down	
Glove	Hold glove out as target in front of body	Holding glove to one side or the other
	Relax hands, give steady target	Arms and hands stiff
	Keep bare hand alongside (slightly behind) glove	

THE CATCHER

Skill	Cue	Common Error
Receiving	Fingers up (pitch above waist)	
	Fingers down (pitch below waist)	
	Block ball in dirt with body	Trying to catch ball in dirt
	Relax hands and draw body in	Arms and hands stiff; unable to cushion ball
	Move body over to get in front of inside or outside pitches	Standing still and trying too reach to one side or the other to catch
Throwing	Get up quickly	Sitting on heels and not getting into throwing position
	Push off ball of back foot, step directly toward target with front foot	

FIELDING

Skill	Cue	Alternate Cue	Common Error
Hard Hit	Catch ball as if it were an egg		
	Give with ball; bring it into waist		Body and hand stiff
Slow Hit	Get behind ball		
	Scoop ball as if with a shovel		
Rolling Ball	Pick and throw	Use hand to pick and throw if time is of essence	Using the glove to "pick" and then throwing
Focus of Eyes	See ball into glove		Looking away
Chin	Keep chin on chest as you go down		Pulling head up too soon

STRAIGHT-IN SLIDE

Skill	Cue	Alternate Cue	Common Error
Approach	Inside corner of base (ball is in outfield)	Approach to infield side of base when throw is coming from outfield	Sliding into plate
	Outside corner of base (ball is in infield)	Approach to outfield side of base when throw is coming from infield	
Sliding Action (Figure 18.5)			
Leg Action	Lead with top leg straight, bottom leg bent under (looks like a figure "4")	Slide on outside of calf and thigh	Not getting bottom leg bent under
Torso Action	Sit down		Sitting straight up
	Lean back, relax back		Body tense
Arms	Touchdown signal	Arms above head (prevents injuries)	Dragging arms, hands, and elbows
Head Position	Back	Eyes on play	Keeping head up, resulting in a tag in face or head
Base Contact	Lead with heel, like stopping a scooter or slide	Sole up	Soles down and getting cleats stuck in dirt
	Straight leg		

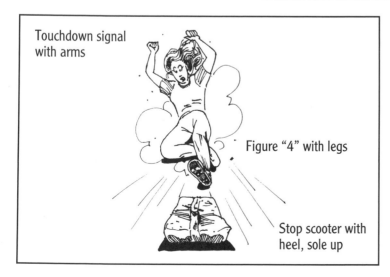

Touchdown signal with arms

Figure "4" with legs

Stop scooter with heel, sole up

FIGURE 18.5 Straight-In Slide.

Chapter 19

Swimming

INTRODUCTION

The swimming and safety cues incorporated in this chapter provide instructors with a variety of creative ideas that students of all ages are able to visualize and implement into their swimming and safety skills. For example, when teaching the prone float, one might instruct the students to pretend they are "Superheroes looking over the city." Other feedback about this cue might be "Look to see if someone is in trouble." Questions could include "How is the person doing down there?" or "Can you see the crooks?" When these cues are used, students' imaginations are stimulated, and critical swimming skills are learned. When teachers use their imaginations with the cues and elaborate on them, the class becomes interesting and fun.

We have designed some very vivid swimming cues to help the swimmer envision the arm stroke, kick, and coordination patterns. For example, making an inverted heart for the breaststroke or an hourglass for the butterfly stroke helps the student learn to perform a difficult arm movement more quickly and efficiently.

Other cues are designed to help refine and polish the strokes—for example, "thumb brushes side of leg on the finish of the front crawl arm stroke" or "hand rests on top of leg to finish the arm stroke on the sidestroke." These refinement cues should be used when the swimmer has mastered major arm, kick, and coordination patterns.

Learning correct swimming strokes through the use of cues helps the student feel more comfortable and efficient in the water, which could lead to a lifetime of fitness and recreational activities.

SKILLS LISTED WITH CUES

Swimming strokes include the following: front crawl, back crawl, butterfly, sidestroke, breaststroke, elementary backstroke, trudgen, trudgen crawl, double trudgen, inverted breaststroke, and overarm sidestroke.

Swimming skills in this chapter are in a teaching progression for Levels I through V, and include (a) floats, glides, and rotary breathing, (b) turns of all kinds, (c) surface dives, (d) safety skills, and (e) diving progressions.

TIPS

1. Type the cues on a 3″ × 5″ card, laminate it, and float the card on the water while teaching.
2. Punch holes in the note card, put string through the holes, and tie a knot. Put string around instructor's neck. The note card won't float away from the swim instructor.
3. For laminating the note card: use clear contact paper, heavy Ziploc bags, clear postal tape.

EQUIPMENT TIPS

1. Goggles help beginning swimmers to enjoy the water and to open their eyes underwater; they also prevent the eyes from burning when a person swims laps.
2. Kickboards.

TEACHING IDEAS

1. The following is a suggested teaching progression for the five basic swimming strokes: front crawl, back crawl, elementary backstroke, breaststroke, and sidestroke. The sidestroke should be taught after the whip kick has been mastered because of negative transfer with the scissors kick.
2. Front crawl: If students have erratic breathing habits or body twists, have them breathe on the opposite side. This tactic helps them to relearn correct breathing patterns.
3. Sidestroke: Have students learn sidestroke on both sides.
4. Breaststroke coordination: When teaching the breaststroke to beginners, have students practice only one stroke. Stop until they master the one stroke, then add two strokes, three strokes, and so on. This method helps develop coordination and gliding for the stroke.
5. Wet base (modified game): A new water game played like baseball in the water.

EQUIPMENT

1 kickboard used for the bat
1 lightweight plastic 8-inch ball
4 hula hoops used for the bases
4 10-pound weights to keep hula hoops secure (optional)

Rules

1. Batter stands in shallow end of pool, bats to deep end of pool; pitcher pitches ball underhand, no more than three pitches.
2. Bat like baseball, swim underwater through hoop to first base, then to second base, and so on. Award one point for making it back to home plate.
3. A ball that goes out on deck is a foul ball.
4. Outs are made just as in baseball.
5. Two teams (4 to 10 per team).

FYI

For further information and special help, consult the following organizations and sources:

Your local American Red Cross

National Headquarters of the American Red Cross
430 17th Street Northwest
Washington, DC 20006
Phone: (202) 737–8300

U.S. Swimming, Inc.
One Olympic Plaza
Colorado Springs, CO 80909
Phone: (719) 578–4578
Fax: (719) 578–4669

American Red Cross. (1993). *CPR for the professional rescuer*. St. Louis, MO: Mosby.

American Red Cross. (1981). *Swimming and aquatics safety*. Washington, DC: The American Red Cross.

American Red Cross. (1992). *Swimming and diving*. St. Louis, MO: Mosby.

Counsilman, J. E. (1977). *Competitive swimming manual for coaches and swimmers*. Bloomington, IN: Counsilman.

Counsilman, J. E., & Counsilman, B. E. (1994). *The new science of swimming*. Englewood Cliffs, NJ: Prentice-Hall.

Fronske, H. (1988). *Relationships among various objective swimming tests and expert evaluations of skill in swimming*. Unpublished dissertation. Brigham Young University, Provo, UT.

FRONT CRAWL

Skill	Cue	Alternate Cue	Common Error
Body Position	Iron rod down back	Be a superhero	Hips and shoulders sway
Head Position	Water level at crown of head		Head too far under the water
			Head too high (creates a drag)
Arm Pull	Use an S pull	Pull up and in, like a sculling motion	Straight arm pull
	Thumb to middle of leg		Hand-first recovery

FRONT CRAWL

Skill	Cue	Alternate Cue	Common Error
Arm Recovery (Figure 19.1)	High elbow recovery	Elbow first, like a string pulling elbow up to ceiling	Dragging elbow in water
	Drag thumb lightly along the water	Fingertips close to water	Straight arm recovery
			Hand is higher than elbow during recovery
Hand Entry	Spear a fish that is 2 to 3 inches below the water and in front of you	Reach with arm	Palm enters the water first
	Try to make a spear with arm		Hand starts to pull too soon
Leg Action	Point toes like a diver	Kick heels to the surface	If feet are flexed stiff, swimmer does not move forward, can even go backward in the water
	Feet relaxed, like throwing a fishing line	Kick generated from large muscles of buttocks and thigh	

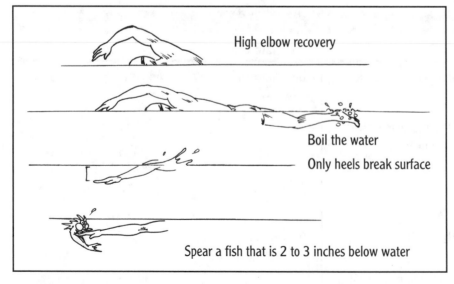

High elbow recovery

Boil the water

Only heels break surface

Spear a fish that is 2 to 3 inches below water

FIGURE 19.1   Front Crawl.

FRONT CRAWL

Skill	Cue	Alternate Cue	Common Error
Breathing	Follow the elbow back; look through window	Roll chin to shoulder	Head too far under the water (causes exaggerated roll)
	Rotate body on skewer	Predominately on side	
	Hum while face is in water	Exhale through nose	Water gets in mouth

BACK CRAWL

Skill	Cue	Alternate Cue	Common Error
Body Position	Iron rod down back		Hips and shoulders sway
Head Position	Lie down, as if head is on a pillow, water touching ears	Eyes look at toes splashing water	Head is too far back, eyes looking at the ceiling
Hand Recovery (Figure 19.2)	Thumb leads coming out of the water as if a string is pulling the thumb up	Thumbs up, like making the OK sign	Fingers lead coming out of the water

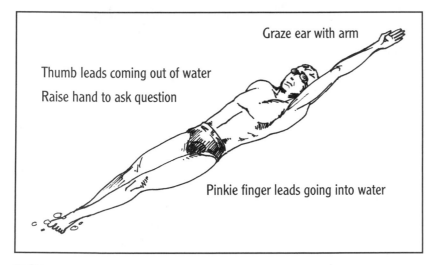

Graze ear with arm

Thumb leads coming out of water

Raise hand to ask question

Pinkie finger leads going into water

FIGURE 19.2 Back Crawl.

BACK CRAWL			
Skill	**Cue**	**Alternate Cue**	**Common Error**
Shoulder Recovery	Lead with shoulder; straight arm Graze your ear with your arm	Raise hand to ask question Skim the ear	Arms are bent
Hand Entry	Pinkie finger always leads going into the water	Palms facing away	Arms enter too far out to the side of the body Hand or elbow enters first
Arm Pull	Make a question mark with each arm pull		Straight arm pull
Leg Action	Point toes like a diver Kick on side	Kick toes to the surface Make water boil	Flexed stiff feet; swimmer does not move forward well, knees and heels break the surface of the water
Body Rotation	Rotate body on skewer	Hip to sky	

BUTTERFLY STROKE			
Skill	**Cue**	**Alternate Cue**	**Common Error**
Arm Pull	Draw an hourglass with high elbow pull Push arms; explode out of the back of stroke; touch thigh with thumb	Draw a keyhole shape with both arms Stay low	Straight arm pull
Arm Recovery	Elbow is being pulled by string upward Thumb drags along the water to keep the elbows high	Pinkies exit first	Elbows stay in water on recovery Arms drag along the water

BUTTERFLY STROKE

Skill	Cue	Alternate Cue	Common Error
Hand Entry	Catch the water with hands	As hands enter in front, chest is down, buttocks up	
Leg Action	Legs are together, like a mermaid		Legs too far apart
	Two strong kicks	Emphasize both upbeat and downbeat	Whip kick or frog kick
	Make kick like a metronome		
Coordination	Lead with head	Head leads the stroke	
	As hands enter in front, chest is down, buttocks up	Hands go in as buttocks go up	
Breathing	Keep chin near the water when breathing		
Body Roll	Body roll through a relatively narrow band of water at surface	No deeper than 1 to 2 feet	

SIDESTROKE

Skill	Cue	Alternate Cue	Common Error
Body Position	Lay head on arm	Stay on side by looking over shoulder of top arm	Ear and head too far above the water
			Lying on stomach
	Lower ear is in water		
Arm Pull	Tie a big knot	Pick an apple from a tree and put it in your pocket	Both hands start above head

SIDESTROKE

Skill	Cue	Alternate Cue	Common Error
Arm Recovery	Rest the top hand on the top leg during the glide	Pat your top leg	Top arm pushes too far past the leg
Leg Action	Tuck the knees, flex the top foot, and point the bottom foot	Draw both heels toward buttocks	Whip or frog kick used
	Do the splits	Splits done sideways	Legs too close together when trying to make the splits, legs go up and down, not sideways
	Legs do not pass each other when kick is finished	Avoid up-and-down splits, close legs like scissors	Legs pass each other on the kick
Coordination	Stay streamlined Count to 3 on glide	Look at the side of pool Stay parallel with side	Roll or lie on stomach

BREASTSTROKE

Skill	Cue	Alternate Cue	Common Error
Body Position	Arch back to bring shoulders out of water	Superhero glide	Body vertical in water
Head Position	Eyes focused on the wall	Crown at water level	Hair submerged in water
Arm Pull/Arm Recovery	Make a small upside down heart; start at the point of the heart, trace it with hand, then split it in half with hands	Scrape sides of a bowl with hands, and put back what you scraped	Heart shape is too wide or long

BREASTSTROKE

Skill	Cue	Alternate Cue	Common Error
Arm Glide	Fully extend arms and count to 3 before starting to pull	Hold arms extended for 2 or 3 seconds	Starting to pull too soon
Leg Action (Whip Kick)	Kick buttocks with heels Try being knock-kneed Draw circles with heels	Knees a fist apart Keep knees closer together than ankles Push feet/squeeze legs	Knees too far apart Frog kick Knees outside ankles
Breathing	Lift chin, not head, to to breathe		Head too far out of water
Coordination	Pull, breathe, kick, glide		Gliding when arms are at waist

ELEMENTARY BACKSTROKE

Skill	Cue	Alternate Cue	Common Error
Body Position	Ears in the water Arms down at sides	Streamlined	Head too far out of water
Arm Recovery	Tickle sides with thumbs all the way to the armpits	Elbows lead thumbs to armpits	Hands do not come to armpits, $\frac{1}{2}$ stroke
Arm Pull	Palms out Make a snow angel	Make a T	Hands and arms come too far above head

ELEMENTARY BACKSTROKE

Skill	Cue	Alternate Cue	Common Error
Leg Action (Whip Kick) (Figure 19.3)	Drop feet straight down	Make penguin feet	Buttocks drop, knees bend to chest
	Try being knock-kneed	Feet outside knees	Knees are outside of ankles
	Upper legs form a table	Draw heels toward buttocks	Knees come out of water
	Try drawing circles with your heels	Push feet, then squeeze legs	Scissors kick with one or both legs
Coordination	Recover the arms first, kick and pull, then glide	Up-out together, glide	Arms and legs start at the same time

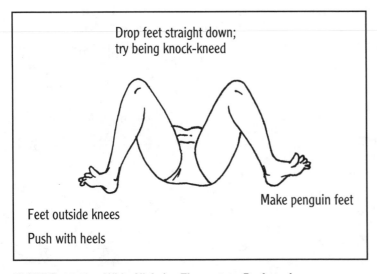

Drop feet straight down; try being knock-kneed

Make penguin feet

Feet outside knees

Push with heels

FIGURE 19.3 Whip Kick for Elementary Backstroke.

SWIMMING SKILLS—LEVELS I AND II

Skill	Cue	Common Error
Entering the Water	Getting into a bathtub; splash arms, legs, face to get adjusted to water temperature	Getting in too fast
Bubble Blowing	Humming—like an alligator's face in water	Mouth open too wide, blowing through mouth
Supported Float on Front	Like being a hang glider	Too tense, not relaxed
Supported Float on Back	Lying on sand looking at sky Belly up	Head too far forward, hips dropped
Supported Kick on Front	Steamboat or boil the water	Feet come too far out of water, feet too deep under water, bicycle kick
Supported Kick on Back	Boil the water	Knees come out of water
Hold Breath and Submerge Head	Be a submarine	Inhaling under water
Orientation to Deep Water	Hold on to side like bunny paws Slide your hands Hug the wall	Letting go with both hands
Prone Float from Standing Position	Be a hinge Kick one leg up and then the other leg	

SWIMMING SKILLS—LEVELS I AND II

Skill	Cue	Common Error
Prone Float or Glide (Figure 19.4)	Superhero Superhero looking over the city Superhero looking for person in trouble	Arms down at side Eyes closed
Supine Float from Standing	Head back, ears in water Push tummy to blue sky Kick one leg up and then the next leg	
Supine Float or Glide	Be a torpedo	Bending at waist or lifting head up
Prone Float to Stand (On Stomach)	Lift head Make a cannonball, push arms down Stand up	Tucking chin Body stays straight Getting off balance

FIGURE 19.4 Streamline Position like a Superhero.

SWIMMING SKILLS—LEVELS I AND II

Skill	Cue	Common Error
Back Float to Stand (On Back)	Tuck chin Cannonball Push feet and arms down Stand up	Head stays back Body stays straight Staying on back
Rhythmic Breathing	Chin to shoulder Blow through nose and mouth	Lifting head up Trying to take a quick breath and then blowing air out above water
Flutter Kick on Front	Superhero/steamboat	Bicycle kick Head too far out of water
Flutter Kick on Back	Lie on sand, toes break water	Knees break water
Finning on Back	Hands like little wings	Arms too tense and jerky
Back Crawl Arm Action	Arms recover straight like a soldier Graze ear/skim ear Pinkie finger enters first	Bent arm recovery Arm too far from ear Palm enters first
Pull Underwater	Make a question mark	Straight arm pull
Combined Stroke on Front	Reach over a barrel Point toes like a diver	Elbow drops Kick too deep, flexed feet
Turning Over Front to Back	Drop one shoulder Roll like a log or hot dog	Drop both feet, shoulders flat

SWIMMING SKILLS—LEVELS I AND II

Skill	Cue	Common Error
Retrieve Object	Try doing a handstand in the water	Too tense
	Reach hand for object	Not bending at waist
Bob in Water to Travel to Safe Area	Jack rabbit moves to wall	Knees stiff
	Kangaroo moves to wall	Jumping up and down in place
Supine Glide with Push-Off	Tuck position on wall, spring off wall like a torpedo	Standing up position
	Ears touch water	Not pushing with feet
Prone Glide with Push-Off	Spring off wall	Not tucking
	Superhero looking over city; look for person in trouble	
	Water level at crown of head	

SWIMMING SKILLS—LEVEL III

Skill	Cue	Common Error
Alternating Arm Action in Back Crawl	One arm up, one arm down, graze ear	Both arms down at side
	Spin arms	Arm action in slow motion
Reverse Direction on Front and Back	Pull harder with inside arm	Pulling with both arms
	Make a U turn	
	Keep kicking to stay on top of water	Not kicking
Deep-Water Bobbing	A frog leaping	Straight legs
	Exhale through nose, like a rocket taking off	Inhaling underwater

SWIMMING SKILLS—LEVEL III

Skill	Cue	Common Error
Buoyancy and Floating Position	Arms above head	Arms at side
	Fingers point to sky	
	Knees bent	Legs straight
	Fill lungs with air	Quick shallow breaths
Rotary Breathing	Hum in water	Open mouth/drink pool
	Bubbles through nose mostly	Not blowing out of nose, water goes up nose
	Chin to shoulder	
Elementary Backstroke Coordination	See Elementary Backstroke cues	
Sculling on Back		
Flat Scull	Figure 8 motion, hands by hips	Arms too stiff
	Palms up, palms down	Hands too close to surface
Head First	Figure 8, fingers point to sky	Arms stiff, body rigid
	Waving up	Fingers point down or flat
		Finning flat
Feet First	Figure 8, fingers point to floor	Arms stiff
	Waving down	Fingers point up or flat
		Straight wrists
Dolphin Kick	Wave with body	Kicking from the knees
	Be a mermaid with feet together	
Scissors Kick	Lying on side, ear in water	Rolling on stomach
	Scissors out, scissors in, cutting the water	Whip kick
	Bring legs together	Crossing legs

SWIMMING SKILLS—LEVEL III

Skill	Cue	Common Error
Rotary Kick (Figure 19.5)	Sit on horse, back straight	Standing straight up
	One foot rotates clockwise, the other foot, counterclockwise	Legs going same direction
	Eggbeater	
	Wax on! Wax off! with your feet (as in the *Karate Kid* movie—same motion, just use feet)	
Tread Water	Look over fence	
Arms	Figure 8 with hands, palms up, palms down or like spreading butter with sides of hands	Hands pushing down
Legs	Scissors/breaststroke/rotary	
Body Position	Relaxed	Body too rigid, not relaxed
		Too much energy, too tight

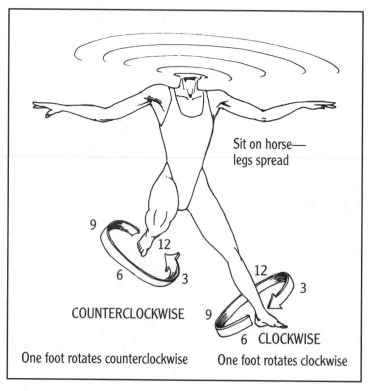

Sit on horse—
legs spread

9
12
6
3

COUNTERCLOCKWISE

12
3
9
6 CLOCKWISE

One foot rotates counterclockwise   One foot rotates clockwise

FIGURE 19.5 Rotary Kick.

SWIMMING SKILLS—LEVEL III

Skill	Cue	Common Error
Front Open Turn	Drop one shoulder, meet hands above head	Grab wall with both hands
	Knees tuck against wall; submerge in water	Not tucking
	Spring off wall	No push
	Stay submerged	Staying on top of water, not submerging
Back Open Turn	Drop one shoulder, meet hands above head	Arms by side
	Spring off wall	Not tucking
	Be a torpedo	No power
Sidestroke Arms and Coordination	See Sidestroke cues	

SWIMMING SKILLS—LEVEL IV

Skill	Cue	Common Error
Swimming Underwater	Be a submarine	Swimming on top of water
	Scrape a big bowl with hands	Straight arm pull
	Be a frog	
Butterfly Arm Stroke and Coordination	See butterfly stroke cues	
Breaststroke Turn	Drop shoulder, hands meet above head; submerge	Shoulders level
	Superhero looking over city underwater	
Sidestroke Turn	Touch wall with leading arm	Touch wall with both arms
	Drop one shoulder	
	Spring off wall	

SWIMMING SKILLS—LEVEL IV

Skill	Cue	Common Error
Speed Turn and Pull Out for Breaststroke	Drop one shoulder, meet hands above head	
	Spring off wall	Not tucked
Arms	Draw light bulb to thighs (feel water move down legs to toes)	Shallow pull
Legs	Whip kick and stretch	Kicking too quick after pull
Flip Turn for Front Crawl	Front somersault (one stroke from edge of pool)	Body stays flat, too far from or too close close to wall
	Bend at waist; be a hinge	
	Put buttocks in air	No tuck
	Throw legs out of water	
	Find wall with feet	Finding wall with buttocks, too close to wall, finding gutter instead
	Put footprints on wall	
Flip Turn for Backstroke	Turn on stomach one stroke from edge	
	Do a front flip turn	
	Push off on back like a torpedo, arms above head	
Pike Surface Dive	Swim with continuous motion into pike; pull water up; drive your head down	No power into pike
	Hands touch toes	Body stays flat
	Be a hinge or break like a pencil at hips	Stay in bent position
	Shoot legs up or put pencil back together as you dive down	
Tuck Surface Dive	Swim front crawl with continuous motion	No power into swim
	Drive your head down; pull water up	
	Swim and roll into ball or cannonball	Head remains up
	Cannonball explodes, shoot feet up in air	

SWIMMING SKILLS—LEVEL IV

Skill	Cue	Common Error
Feet-First Surface Dive		
Arm Action	Start in T position	Starting with hands at side
	Perform jumping jack action with arms	
	Arms and hands push down like a jumping jack and push back up like a jumping jack	
	or	
	Push arms back up like a referee's signal for a touchdown	Keeping arms down at side

TRUDGEN STROKES

Skill	Cue	Common Error
Trudgen	Front crawl	Breathing on both sides
	Roll hips to side	Whip kick staying on stomach
	Scissors kick when breathing	Kicking when head is in water
Trudgen Crawl	Front crawl	
	Roll hip to side	Hips flat
	Scissors kick when breathing, flutter kick when face is in water	Forgetting to flutter kick
	Breathe on one side	
Double Trudgen	Front crawl with no flutter kick	
	Scissors kick—scissors kick	Kicking only one side
	Roll hip to each side when performing a scissors kick on each arm stroke	Not rolling hips
	Breathe on one side only	Breathing on both sides
	Head stays in water on one arm stroke and one scissors kick; keep head in water	Turning head right and left
	Try to keep arms moving and in sequence with each scissors kick	

WATER ENTRIES AND SAFETY SKILLS

Skill	Cue	Common Error
Stride Jump	Hug water	Grabbing air with arms
	Scoop at water	Moving arms together before they land in water
	Split with legs	
	Cut water with legs	Legs together too soon
	Lean forward	Standing straight up, jumping in
Feet-First Jump Entry	Hold head erect	Head down
	Keep eyes on victim	Eyes down
	Spread arms and legs quickly	
	Cross ankles to prevent injury to groin	Not crossing ankles
Release of Cramp	Try to relax and change swimming stroke	Panicking and tightening the muscle even more
Deep Water	Take a deep breath	Drinking pool
	Roll face down	Keeping head up
	Extend leg, flex foot, like touching toes	
	Massage cramp	
Help	Fetal position	Lying flat
	Head up	
	Arms and legs crossed	Arms and legs at side
Huddle	Touching shoulders	Too far apart
	Group hug	
	Put smallest individual in middle of circle	

SWIMMING SKILLS—LEVEL V

Skill	Cue	Common Error
Swimming in Clothing		
Rules	Keep clothes on if water is cold	
Shoes and Socks	Remove shoes and socks first if too heavy	
Strokes to Use	Breaststroke	
	Elementary backstroke	
	Sidestroke	
Inflating Clothing	Tuck shirt in or tie shirt	Front of shirt not underwater
Shirt	Fasten top button, undo second or third button, and blow in	
	Pull shirt up to face and blow in like blowing up a balloon	
	Inflate shirt or jacket by splashing air into it	
Reaching Assists		
Talking to Victim	Let victim know he or she has been seen	Not communicating with victim, verbal or nonverbal
	Give victim directions to help him or her help you	
	Ask the victim to move forward to you by kicking and moving arms	
Out of Water	Firmly brace yourself on deck	
	Reach out to victim with object; for example, arm, towel, kickboard, shepherd's crook, branch, belt	Throwing object at victim's head
	Make sure victim grasps object	
	Lean on back leg, pull slowly	Leaning forward or keeping both feet together
In Water	Hold on to pool, ladder, trough, or other secure object	Releasing grasp on edge
	Extend free hand or leg	Swimming out to victim
	Grasp victim's wrist and pull in	Victim grasps you

SWIMMING SKILLS—LEVEL V

Skill	Cue	Common Error
Reaching Assists *(cont.)*		
Throwing Assists	Get into stride position, bend knees	Standing tall
	Step on line	Forgetting to step on line
	Throw beyond victim	Throwing at victim or in front of victim
	When victim grasps object lean back, like pulling on a tug-of-war rope	Letting go of rope with both hands
Human Chain	Interlock wrists	Holding hands
	Every other person is facing same direction like a zipper	All facing same direction
Shallow-Water	Side to side/pool or beach/small victim	Facing victim
	Position right hand around victim's waist	Arm position wrong
	Rescuer puts head under victim's left arm	
	Grasp victim's left arm	Not walking slowly enough
Drag	Behind victim/shore or beach/heavy victim	Standing to side of victim
	Grasp under armpits	Locking hands around victim
	Drag victim to shore	Not using legs
Deep-Water Lift* (do not use if you suspect a spinal injury)	Grab victim's wrists, put one hand on top of other	Not staying behind victim
	Rescuer places hand on top of victim's hands	Letting go of victim's hands
	Get out from side, then face victim	Letting go of victim when getting out
	Grasp wrist firmly, stand close to edge, bend knees and lift victim	Straight legs

*Not to be used if spinal injury is suspected.

DIVING

Skill	Cue	Common Error
Safety Rules	Dive in water deep enough (9 feet or over)	Diving in less than 9 feet of water can cause spinal injuries or head injuries
	Obstructions when diving should be at least 4 feet on either side of the diver	Less than 4 feet on either side of the diver
Side of Pool Dive *Kneeling Position*	Kneel on one knee; grip pool edge with other foot	Kneeling on two knees
	Head between arms and fingers pointing to water	Hands and arms moving to front of body
	Focus on target on bottom 4 feet out or surface 1 to 2 feet from side	Not focusing on target (causes a belly flop)
Action of Dive	Lean forward, try to touch water	Jumping in water with head lifted
	Push with front foot	Somersaulting in
	Keep hips up and dive over barrel	Hips down
	Straighten legs	Legs bent
	Push downward in water with hands	Pushing upward
Compact Dive	One foot forward, one foot back	Staying on knee
	Kneel and rise	Staying on knee
	Head between arms, point fingers at water	Head not between arms
	Hips up, stretch and touch surface of water	Hips down, hands in air
	Lose balance, push off toward water	
	Ankles together on water entry	Legs apart
Stride Dive	Walking stance	Legs together
	Front toes grab edge	Foot is not at edge
	Head between arms	Head is up
	Bend at the waist like breaking a pencil	Body is straight
	Kick back leg up, hips up	Not kicking leg
	Once body is underwater, point fingers to surface of water	Fingers pointed down

DIVING		
Skill	**Cue**	**Common Error**
Side of Pool Dive (cont.)		
Long Shallow Dive	Push and stretch	Falling in or plopping in
	Spear into the water	Pointing fingers to bottom of pool
	Over the barrel and through the hoop	
	Hands enter through doughnut hole	
	Go through the tunnel just below surface of water	
Diving from the Board	Hips up, arms stretched, fall forward, focus on target in water	Hips down
Approach Hurdle	Lift knee like a tabletop or a stork position	Keeping knee down
	Arms back, like pushing ski poles	
	Arms up to touchdown position	Arms staying down
Jump off Board	Use approach hurdle position	One or two steps in approaching hurdle
	Arms back like a back arm circle	
	Land on two feet and push off board	
Jump, Tuck Position	Use approach hurdle position	
	Jump off board	
	Lift knees to chest in fetal position; straighten back up in spear position	Not getting in a tuck position
Tuck Dive	Use approach hurdle position	
	Jump in tuck position	
	Lift hips	Hips down
	Drive heels into ceiling	
	Push hands into water, above head	Hands down
Pike Dive	Use approach hurdle position	
	Hips up	Hips down
	Break the pencil	Bending at hips
	Fingers to toes	
	Drive heels into ceiling	

Chapter 20

Team Handball

INTRODUCTION

Although a popular Olympic sport for men and women throughout the world, team handball is an emerging sport in the United States that often suffers from an identity crisis. Most of the world calls the game "handball," but in the United States there is already another sport with that name. When most Americans hear "team handball" mentioned, they mistakenly envision a game like racquetball, played on a court and involving hitting a small black ball with both hands. Without a doubt, team handball is *not off the wall!*

Team handball is a dynamic sport that is fun to play and exciting to watch. Natural athletic skills such as running, jumping, throwing, and catching provide the action for the game. Players and spectators alike enjoy the fast continuous play, body contact, and goalie action. First-time spectators describe team handball as soccer with your hands, but they also notice elements that remind them of basketball, water polo, and ice hockey.

Team handball is played between two teams, each with six court players and a goalie, on a court larger than a basketball court. The object of the game is to throw a cantaloupe-sized ball into the opponent's 2-meter-by-3-meter goal and defend one's own goal from attack. A regulation game is played in 30-minute halves with no time-outs. A coin toss determines which team starts the game with a throw-off. From that point, the action is continuous. The clock stops only for injury or at the referee's discretion. A successful scoring attempt results in the award of one point. Goals scored per game typically range from the upper teens to midtwenties.

A semicircular line 6 meters from the goal marks the goal area. Only the goalie occupies this area, and both attackers and defenders must remain outside. Basic defense is designed to protect the goal area by placing all six players around it forming a wall. Defense techniques are similar to basketball with the exception that more contact is allowed. Body contact with the torso is permitted, but players may not push, hold, or endanger an opponent in any way. Excessive roughness results in two-minute suspensions.

When in attack, players are called back courts, wings, and circle runners. Passing is the primary way to move the ball in attack. A player is allowed three steps with the ball before and after dribbling, but while stationary may hold the ball only three seconds. The attacking player's task is to find a way over, around, or through the defensive "wall." This is done by strategies similar to basketball, incorporating the concepts of the "give and go," screen, pick and roll, and overload. The offense may run set plays, but a freelance style usually dominates.

SKILLS LISTED WITH CUES

The cues listed for team handball include passing and catching (overhand pass, catching on the run), individual movement in attack (piston movement and side stepping), shooting (general principles, set shot, jump shot), goalkeeping, defense (basic stance, individual tactics, shot blocking, small-group tactics, team defense: 6–0 zone), offense (attacking the gap, small-group tactics, team offense: fast break, 3–3 formation), and essential team handball rules.

TIPS

1. Write or call the United States Team Handball Federation (see FYI) to order the *Introduction to Team Handball* video, a televised game from the Olympics, and basic rules.
2. Set up the VCR and TV in the gym the week before you begin a team handball unit. Show the *Introduction* video and five minutes of the game video the first day of class.
3. Give each student a handout of the simplified rules.
4. Let students experience the game right away with just a few basic team handball rules using skills they already know from other sports like basketball and softball. Add rules as the game develops.
5. After a goal is scored, the goalie puts the ball back into play right away. As a result, the defense must move back quickly. If the court is small, this practice allows more playing area than would be available if the throw-off were made at half-court.
6. Call plenty of 7-meter penalty throws on major fouls, and let the player who was fouled take the throw (a major foul is one that destroys a sure chance to score or any dangerous play, i.e., pushing, tripping, hitting, undercutting a jumping opponent, or grabbing an opponent's arm). This approach helps keep the game safe, and players will learn faster about serious fouls, clear chances to score, and dangerous play.

EQUIPMENT TIPS

1. Regulation indoor court, 20 meters by 40 meters, approximately 65 feet by 131 feet, one-third larger than a basketball court.
2. Indoors with limited space, that is, only a regulation or smaller basketball court:
   a. Try to maintain 18- to 20-meter width by using extra space outside basketball court.
   b. Small basketball court: Have no sideline boundaries, and play balls off the side walls. Reduce players to five plus a goalie.
   c. After a goal, goalie puts ball back into play with throw-off from the goal area rather than restarting from center court. Goalie cannot leave area or shoot.
3. Outdoor court: playground, grass field, sand beach. For continuous action put an extra ball and student "chaser" behind each goal. Goalie picks up extra ball when shot goes over end line, and student chases the other ball and returns it behind the goal.
4. Marking the court: The most essential lines are the arced 6-meter goal area line and the 7-meter penalty throw line. Use gym floor tape, basketball court three-point line, cones, rope, "chalk dust," paint, or white flour on grass. The dashed free throw line is optional.
5. Modified goals, 2-meter-by-3-meter opening: Tape on wall, portable standards made with rope or old volleyball nets, large crash mat against wall, field hockey or indoor soccer goals, goals built from PVC pipe.

6. Team handballs (about 23 inches in circumference): For safety reasons, the official men's or women's leather ball is not recommended for beginning players or coed classes. Use Sportime's "Supersafe Elite" handball, a dense foam ball, or a slightly deflated volleyball.

TEACHING IDEAS

1. Teach noncontact basketball-style defense. The official handball rules do allow some body contact, but it is not recommended for beginning players.
2. Use the "teaching rules" during scrimmage to encourage players to develop passing and shooting skills along with increasing goalie safety:
   a. Three passes before the team can shoot.
   b. No dribbling or a limited number of dribbles.
   c. Shoot only bounce shots or play without a goalie in the goal area using targets in the goal corners, that is, towels, cones, hoops, and the like. Only the designated goalie can go into goal area and put ball into play after a shot.

FYI

For further information and special help, consult the following organizations:

Team Handball: Step to Success by R. Clanton and M. P. Dwight (release date Fall, 1996). To place an order, call Human Kinetics—toll free 1–800–747–4457.

The authors, physical education teachers/coaches and 1984 Olympians, present an illustrated 12-step progressive program of basic skills and strategies. An excellent teacher resource including drills for increasing and decreasing difficulty of skills, lead-up games, a student rule handout, and more.

U.S. Team Handball Federation
One Olympic Plaza
Colorado Springs, CO 80909
Phone: (719) 578–4582
Fax: (719) 475–1240

Available resources for sale: team handball basic rules sheet; team handball rule book; videos: ask for video listing; suggestions: *Introduction to Team Handball*, Olympic games, international games (designate men's or women's).

Special Olympics International
Sports Department
1325 G Street, Northwest, Suite 500
Washington, DC 20005–3104
Phone: (202) 628–3630 for price and ordering information
Order: Team handball Special Olympics volunteer coach training school manual

FYI

Continued

Suggested equipment companies:

1. Sportime
   Supersafe Elite Handball (6¾″), practice/portable goals, and goal nets
   Phone: 1–800–283–5700

2. Fold-A-Goal
   Practice, portable goals recommended for school programs
   Phone: (213) 734–2507

3. Jayfro
   Folding regulation goals and goal nets
   Phone: (860) 447–3001

PASSING AND CATCHING

Skill	Cue	Common Error
Overhand Pass	Pass with one hand, catch with two	
Preparation	Fingertip grip	Holding ball in palm of hand
	Lift ball up and back with elbow flexed at 90 degrees	Elbow too close to body—ball too close to head
	Weight on back foot	
	Shoulders perpendicular to target	
Throwing Action	Step toward target	
	Rotate and square shoulders to target	No shoulder rotation—always facing target
	Lead with elbow; whip forearm and snap wrist	The ball is pushed from shoulder and hand, and ball leads

PASSING AND CATCHING

Skill	Cue	Common Error
Catching on the Run (Figure 20.1)		
Preparation	Maintain running rhythm	Stopping to catch ball
Position	Hands up, form a triangle with thumbs and forefingers almost touching	
	Push off one leg, extend arms toward ball	
Receiving Action	Soft hands—catch while flexing elbows to give with ball	Ball rebounds off hands
	Land on other foot	

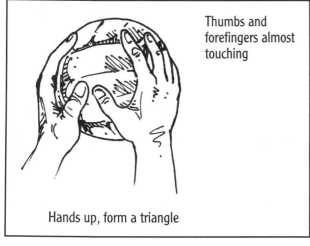

Thumbs and forefingers almost touching

Hands up, form a triangle

FIGURE 20.1   Catching on the Run.

INDIVIDUAL MOVEMENT IN ATTACK

Skill	Cue	Common Error
Piston Movement	Fundamental movement of backcourt players; sum of three actions similar to up-and-down motion of a piston in a motor cylinder	
The Three Actions	1. Run to receive; catch ball while running toward goal	Standing in one spot to receive pass
	2. Use three steps to attack goal; rules: allow three steps with ball (i.e., a right-hander should step left–right–left); on third step, shoot or pass, throw off foot that is opposite to throwing arm	Throwing off foot on same side as throwing arm, or passing ball while backing up
	3. Back up quickly—prepare to attack again	Forgetting to back up and staying too close to defense
Side Stepping	Fundamental movement for circle runners along or near 6-meter line	
Position	Balanced position, knees bent, feet shoulder-width apart, hands open ready to catch	Standing upright with hands down, not ready to catch
Leg Action	Step sideways using quick small steps without crossing feet, maintain balanced position	Bringing feet together or crossing feet

SHOOTING

Skill	Cue	Common Error
General Principles	1. Shoot on move—piston movement	
	2. Watch goalie and shoot for open corners of goal—one may choose to bounce ball when shooting low	
	3. Take shots between 6 and 9 meters; avoid shooting from severe angles	Shooting a set shot from a wing position
	4. Shoot only when there is an opening (shoot over and between defenders)	Charging into a defender or carelessly shooting a ball that hits a stationary defender

SHOOTING		
Skill	**Cue**	**Common Error**
Set Shot		
Preparation	Run to receive and attack using three steps	Standing still when shooting
	Weight on back foot (same as shooting arm)	Shooting off same foot as shooting arm
	Elbow flexed at 90 degrees or greater	
	Shoulders perpendicular to goal	Facing target, shoulders square to goal
	Head up and eyes on goalie, shoot to open corner—equals "cobwebs"	
Throwing Action	Step forward transferring weight from rear to front foot	
	Rotate and square shoulders to goal	
	Lead with elbow, whip forearm, and snap wrist	Pushing ball forward from shoulder
Follow-Through	Momentum continues forward and arm motion continues across body	
Jump Shot	Use jump shot to shoot over a defender, or when jumping into the goal area to score	
Preparation	Run to receive and attack using three steps	

SHOOTING

Skill	Cue	Common Error
Jump Shot *(cont.)*		
Jumping Action (Figure 20.2)	To jump: plant foot opposite throwing arm and drive other knee up (changing forward momentum into upward momentum)	Charging into defender
	Raise shooting arm up and back; make an L	
	Rotate shoulders square to goal, while whipping throwing arm forward (elbow, shoulder, forearm, wrist)	
Throwing Action	Pike slightly at waist and land on takeoff foot	Shot lacks velocity, all power coming from strong upper body action

Raise shooting arm up and back; make an L

Drive knee up

Plant foot opposite throwing arm

FIGURE 20.2   Jump Shot.

GOALKEEPING

Skill	Cue	Common Error
Rules	Goalie is not permitted to 1. Leave goal area while in possession of ball (free throw) 2. Receive a pass from a court player while inside the goal area (penalty throw)	
Goal Throw	Stand inside the goal area and throw ball to a teammate Goal throw is awarded when 1. Ball is blocked and recovered in goal area 2. Blocked ball goes over the end line 3. Ball is thrown over end line by attacking team	
Goalie Protection	Train all beginning players in basic goalie technique—make sure each player gets a chance to play the position Play with a dense foam ball at beginning level Wear long sleeves and pants Males wear a protective cup	
Basic Position (Figure 20.3)	Stand tall with knees slightly flexed, weight on balls of feet, hands up, eyes on ball (like a jumping jack)	Bending at waist with hands low, similar to basketball defensive position
Movement in Goal	Step out about ½ meter from goal line and follow ball by moving with quick shuffle steps, keeping body aligned with the ball Get stable prior to shot, ready to block shot	Standing in middle of goal and not moving Feeling off balance when shot is taken

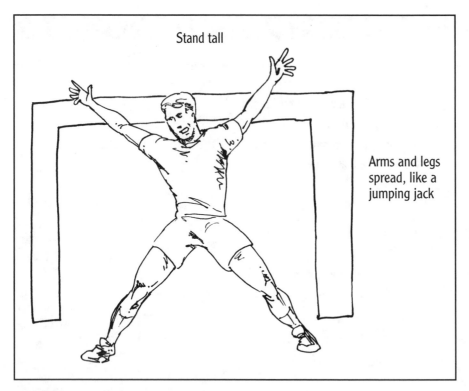

Stand tall

Arms and legs spread, like a jumping jack

FIGURE 20.3   Basic Position of the Goalie.

GOALKEEPING		
Skill	**Cue**	**Common Error**
Blocking High Shots		
Footwork	Take small step in direction of ball, push off leg farthest from ball, and leap in direction of shot	Leaning, reaching for ball rather than moving body
Blocking Action	Extend arm(s) in path of ball and attack the ball—block ball, don't try to catch it	Ball goes through hands when trying to catch it
Blocking Low Shots		
Footwork	Take small step in direction of ball, push off leg farthest from ball	
Blocking Action	Extend opposite leg and arm(s) in path of ball to block	Shot goes over leg—failing to block with both leg and arm(s)

GOALKEEPING

Skill	Cue	Common Error
Blocking Wing Shots		
Position	Stand tall close to goalpost, with weight on goalpost-side leg	
	Goalpost-side arm up, elbow bent at about 90 degrees with forearm in front of face, other hand out to side bent at about 90 degrees	
Footwork	As shooter jumps into the goal area, take one step out from the post and move with quick shuffle steps to keep body aligned with ball	
Blocking Action	Block high shots with arm(s) and low shots with leg and arm(s)	

DEFENSE

Skill	Cue	Common Error
Individual Basic Stance	Feet shoulder-width apart, knees slightly bent, weight forward on balls of feet, body upright, arms out, hands up	Upper body bent forward, hands down, like basketball defensive stance
Individual Defense Tactics		
Movement	Shift along 6-meter line in direction of ball	
	See ball and direct opponent at all times	
	When your opponent attacks, step out from 6-meter line to meet attack— play basketball defense, no contact	Attacker is able to get a shot off from 7 or 8 meters
	Wing defenders should not step out, as a set shot or jump shot is not likely to be successful from such a bad angle	Attacker drives around player and jumps into goal area for a shot
	Stay between opponent and goal	
	When opponent passes the ball, recover to the 6-meter line	Leaving space for circle runner to run behind you

DEFENSE

Skill	Cue	Common Error
Shot Blocking		
Action	From basic stance, extend one or both hands into path of ball	
	Attack ball similar to volleyball blocking	Ball goes through hands toward goal
Small-Group Defense Tactics	Help triangle—when a player steps out, two adjacent players squeeze in slightly for help on both sides	Big open space is left along 6-meter line
	Communicate—each defender should know who is stepping out, who is who is staying back to help	Two players step out to meet one attacker, or no one steps out to meet attacker
Team Defense		
6–0 Zone	All six defenders take positions along 6-meter line forming movable wall in front of goal	
	Shift as a unit in direction of ball movement	
	Each defender is responsible for attacker in his/her area of zone—each attacker should be accounted for by one defender	One defender guarding two attackers, or an attacker left unguarded

OFFENSE		
Skill	**Cue**	**Common Error**
Individual Offense Tactics		
Attack Gap: Space Between Two Defenders	Use fakes to get in a gap	Attacking too close to defenders—causing free throws, which interrupt flow of attack
	Create a workable space from defense	
	Be a threat to score—look to shoot first, then pass	
	Break through gap for a shot from 6-meter line	
	Create overload by drawing two defenders and passing to an open teammate	
Small-Group Offense Tactics	Two or three players work together to create scoring opportunity	
Basketball-Type Tactics	Give and go	
	Pick and roll	
	Crossing	
	Screens	

OFFENSE		
Skill	**Cue**	**Common Error**
Three Phases of Team Offense		
Fast Break	Primary—long pass from goalie to breaking wing	
	Secondary—goalie shoots outlet pass, and team moves ball up floor quickly	
Organize into 3–3 Offense Formation; Move Ball in Support Points	Three players near the 6-meter line:	
	Left wing (LW)	
	Right wing (RW)	
	Circle runner (CR)	
	Three players outside 9-meter line in back court:	
	Left back court (LB)	
	Center back court (CB)	
	Right back court (RB)	
	Move ball with short, quick passes, wing to wing	
	Run to receive, play in good timing with teammates	
Execute Small-Group Tactics	Play with patience, wait for good scoring opportunity	Trying to score too often one-on-one

ESSENTIAL RULES

Skill	Cue	Common Error
Goal-Area Line or 6-Meter Line	The most important line on court No one is allowed inside area except goalie, although players may jump or dive into area prior to releasing ball	
Players	Six court players, one goalie per team Throw-off starts the game and is repeated after every score Offensive team lines up on center line—defense at least 3 meters away Offense passes from center of court to teammate, and play begins	
Playing the Ball	Player is allowed to 1. Run three steps (violation = free throw) 2. Hold ball 3 seconds (violation = free throw) 3. Dribble with no limit, with three steps allowed before and after dribbling (no double dribble) Player is *not* allowed to 1. Throw a ball that endangers opponent 2. Pull, grab, or punch ball out of opponent's hands	
Defending an Opponent	For beginners, noncontact basketball-style defense	

ESSENTIAL RULES

Skill	Cue	Common Error
Throw-In	Awarded when ball goes out of bounds on sideline or when ball is last touched by defensive player (excluding goalie).	
	Place one foot on sideline to throw in	
	Defense 3 meters away	
Free Throw (Minor Fouls and Violations)	Awarded to the opponents at exact spot foul or violation occurred	
	Defense must be 3 meters away; if foul or violation occurs within 3 meters of goal area line, put ball into play at 9-meter line (free throw line)	
	Thrower must keep one foot in contact with floor	
7-Meter Penalty Throw (Major Foul)	Awarded at 7-meter line when a foul destroys a clear chance to score	
	One-on-one shot with the goalie	
	All other players behind the 9-meter line (free throw line)	

Chapter 21

Tennis

INTRODUCTION

Tennis is a game of motion that provides players with a good and enjoyable anaerobic and aerobic workout. Tennis will also improve a player's coordination, agility, foot speed, and reaction time. Tennis skills are relatively easy to learn if proper instruction is given. Three major instructional goals should be adopted by the instructor: (1) spend as little time as possible chasing the ball, (2) keep the frustration level of the student to a minimum, and (3) keep it simple. Tennis also is a mental game that requires the players to be knowledgeable about offensive and defensive maneuvers.

Beginning players often become frustrated with the game and quit because they do not achieve the skill level required to connect with the ball. Most of their time is spent chasing the ball. The tennis instructor's first goal, then, is to get players to hit the ball into the court. Tennis can be a very intimidating sport to teach, but with the help of the right cues and good drills, instructors and students can go away winners and have fun playing the game.

SKILLS LISTED WITH CUES

Included in this chapter are simple instructional cues for the ready position, forehand/backhand ground strokes, two-handed backhand, forehand/backhand volley, lob, drop shot, serving, receiving service, topspin and backspin, overhead smash, doubles and singles strategies, and scoring. These cues are listed in a recommended teaching progression.

TIPS

1. Hit the ball in front of the body for all ground strokes, volleys, half volleys, serves, and overheads.
2. Make immediate out/in calls and signals. Raised index finger indicates "good"; waving the hand next to the knee is the "out" sign.
3. Server says the score after every point, for example, "30–love" (server's score is given first).
4. No swearing, racquet throwing, display of temper, and the like. Encourage good losers as well as graceful winners. Sports reveal your character; play accordingly.
5. Differentiate between failure and mistakes.
6. Forget bad shots immediately; internalize positively.

EQUIPMENT TIPS

1. Be sure the racquet fits the player's hand (fingers need to be ¼ inch away from pad of thumb).
2. Ninety-five percent of the game is hard work and practice, not the equipment you buy.

TEACHING IDEAS

1. Instructional goals can be accomplished by modifying the game for instructional purposes. For example, allow pairs of students to throw balls to each other, instead of both players hitting back and forth.
2. Let the ball bounce more than once so that the hitter can get into position to hit the ball back. Use drills that allow the teacher to throw 5–10 consecutive balls to the student. When students have had their turn, they can retrieve the balls they have hit and put them into the basket for the next student to hit.
3. Forehand only, backhand only, forehand/backhand only, deep court games. Emphasize in these games that when in trouble, "lob the ball" (two-bounce rule used).
4. No singles or doubles second serve when playing games. Service faults are an inefficient use of time. They reduce intensity and concentration.
5. Each player serves 10 balls; play games to 11 points.

FYI

For further information and special help, consult the following organization:

U.S. Tennis Association (USTA)
70 West Red Oak Lane
White Plains, NY 10604
Phone: (914) 696–7000
Fax: (914) 696–7167

FOREHAND STROKE

Skill	Cue	Alternate Cue	Common Error
Ready Position	Feet shoulder-width apart, knees bent Stand on balls of feet Hands in front of belly button, racquet up	Basketball triple-threat position	Racquet drooping down Racquet at side of body Flat-footed
Grip	Shake hands	V shape on top bevel	Squeezing too tightly "Hammer grip"
Racquet Preparation	Turn and step; racquet goes back to hip Hips and shoulders perpendicular to net	Pivot and step	Standing stationary; racquet is in front of body
Flat Stroke (Figure 21.1)	Hand and arm form Y Hold arm in a cast, wrists firm	Racquet back to hip Stroke along a bench	Racquet drooping Elbow bent

Wrist firm

Arm in a cast

Pivot and step

Look at words on ball while it comes to you

FIGURE 21.1 Forehand Stroke.

FOREHAND STROKE

Skill	Cue	Alternate Cue	Common Error
Flat Stroke (cont.)	Arm straight forward, as if painting a straight line on the wall	Like hitting several balls in a row	Snapping wrist Breaking wrist
	Contact is made even with left hip	Wait for ball to drop to hip height	Stationary, waiting for ball
	Hit ball on rise		Hitting ball too high
	Focus on letters or numbers on ball as it comes toward you	Look at the ball, read it (Wilson, Penn, etc.) as it comes to you	Losing focus, daydreaming
		Anticipate where ball will land, watch ball hit string	Turning wrist, relaxing grip
	Finish racquet on edge		

BACKHAND STROKE

Skill	Cue	Alternate Cue	Common Error
Grip	Turn racquet clockwise	Make V on left bevel	Failure to rotate grip from forehand to backhand
	Knuckle on top	First knuckle on top of racquet	Rotating racquet counterclockwise
Stance	Turn and step	Pivot and step	Stationary
	Right hip and shoulder perpendicular to net		
Stroke (Figure 21.2)	Pull sword from scabbard		Not getting racquet back Swinging level
	Ball contact made at hip level; power originates here	Contact made in front of right hip	Contacting ball too high
	Sweep, swing, or stroke through ball	Wait for ball to drop knee-high	Poking or jabbing at ball

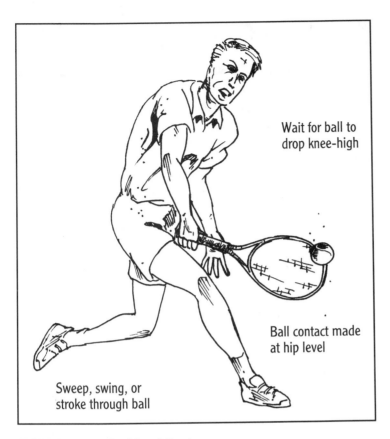

Wait for ball to
drop knee-high

Ball contact made
at hip level

Sweep, swing, or
stroke through ball

FIGURE 21.2   Backhand Stroke.

BACKHAND STROKE			
Skill	**Cue**	**Alternate Cue**	**Common Error**
Follow-Through	Grab racquet out in front with second hand		Aborting follow-through
Two-Handed Stroke	Left hand pushes racquet through swing	Push racquet through with left hand	Not worrying about gripping racquet with left hand
	Right hand takes a backhand grip		Not rotating racquet
	Hit ball as if stroking through a long tube	Hit ball through a long rifle barrel	Poking or jabbing at ball

VOLLEY STROKES

Skill	Cue	Alternate Cue	Common Error
Forehand (Figure 21.3)	Step, punch, make quarter moon	Ready position already established, step and punch	Rushing shot, swinging
	Hand below ball	Racquet face looks straight ahead/flat stroke	
	Firm wrist, firm grip		Wrist not firm
			Like windshield wiper action, breaking wrist
	Shoulders face net		Shoulders facing sideways
	Racquet never goes behind front shoulder	Keep racquet in peripheral vision	Racquet goes behind back shoulder

Firm wrist, firm grip
when ball contacts racquet

NET .

Hand below ball

Step and punch

FIGURE 21.3 Forehand Volley.

VOLLEY STROKES

Skill	Cue	Alternate Cue	Common Error
Backhand	Step, punch, make quarter moon	Ready position already established, step and punch	Not swinging
	Hand below ball	Squat to get to ball	Hand above ball
	Firm wrist/grip; elbow down		Elbow up
	Racquet never goes behind front shoulder	Keep racquet in peripheral vision	Racquet goes behind back shoulder
Two-Handed Backhand	Both hands on grip		Swinging at ball
	Step/short swing or punch		Full backswing and forward swing
	Racquet never goes behind front shoulder		Trying to hit like a regular forehand and backhand stroke

LOB AND DROP SHOT

Skill	Cue	Alternate Cue	Common Error
Lob	Rotate racquet opposite of backhand		
	Swing low to high	Soft touch	Hitting ball too hard
	Pull racquet arm to opposite shoulder	Aim forward and upward, doing both things at same time	No follow-through
Offensive	Lob must be height of fence; lob over fence		Not aiming lob
	Hit to big square		Lob too short; not following through
	Clear fence (good practice height)		
Drop Shot Slice	Act like hitting a back-hand or forehand but cut shot in half	Soft touch at contact	Full follow-through

SERVE			
Skill	**Cue**	**Alternate Cue**	**Common Error**
Toss (Figure 21.4)	Hold ball at shoulder level		Holding ball too low Bringing ball down to knee
	Pinch the ball with pads of fingertips (flat ball, no spin)	Hold an egg	Ball touching pinkie finger (causes spin)
	Toss ball 1 foot above release position for throwing		Pushing ball up with palm of hand
	Extend arm fully, like elevator lift to top floor	Elevate hand to Statue of Liberty position	Elbow bent
	Practice tossing ball under a basketball hoop, pipe, or tube; ball goes up through cylinder	Practice standing by fence post; toss directly up fence post	Hand elevated behind head or pushed too far out in front of face
	Ball should land 1 foot from front toe		Tossing ball behind, in front, to left or right of head

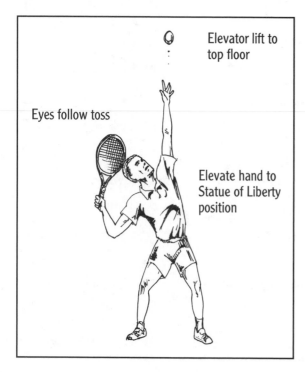

Elevator lift to top floor

Eyes follow toss

Elevate hand to Statue of Liberty position

FIGURE 21.4   Toss for the Serve.

SERVE			
Skill	**Cue**	**Alternate Cue**	**Common Error**
Position	Standing on deuce side of court, point left foot at the right net post, left foot forward, right foot back	Everything the same for the ad court serving, except left foot parallel to baseline	Foot fault (server steps on or over baseline before ball strikes racquet)
	Left foot remains stationary	Stand comfortably	
	Back foot doesn't matter		
	Tossing shoulder faces direction to be hit		
	Server focuses on ball while tossing		Viewing opponent(s), or spectators
	Eyes follow toss		Watching receiver dance (breaking concentration on toss)
Action	Racquet is an extension of your arm		Using only shoulder to hit ball
	Visualize yourself as a baseball player	Same action as an outfielder throwing a ball	Punching ball to court
	Throw ball into court		Jabbing at ball
	Reach for ball	Contact is high and in front (contact as high as possible)	Reaching behind head
	Snap wrist (like a whip)		Firm wrist
	Follow-through (racquet finishes by opposite calf)	To get players weight into serve, back foot comes forward to break fall	Hitting and stopping

SERVE

Skill	Cue	Common Error
Let	Ball hits top of net, goes over net into court; serve is taken over again	Calling it a fault or double fault (on first or second serve)
Ace	Serve is in and receiver cannot touch it	
Double Fault	Neither of two serves goes into court	

RECEIVING SERVE

Skill	Cue	Alternate Cue	Common Error
Powerful Serve	Short backswing Block ball	Watch ball go into racquet Like a volley	Bringing racquet too far back Overhitting Big follow-through
Less Powerful Serve	Hit ball into court		
Not a Powerful Serve	Attack net		

SPIN AND SMASH SHOTS

Skill	Cue	Alternate Cue	Common Error
Topspin	Racquet swings low to high	Racquet head perpendicular	Swinging level
	Candy cane swing	J swing	
	Racquet starts knee high and finishes nose high	Shake hands with a friend, and finish shaking hands with a giant	
Backspin (Slice) (Figure 21.5)	Racquet swings high to low	Racquet is tilted back	Swinging level
	Cut through ball		
Overhead Smash	Hit like the serve	Refer to serve action	
	Racquet back to neck		
	Left foot in front— power with left foot		Power comes from both feet or back foot
	Point elbow to ball with left hand		Misjudging ball by losing focus of ball

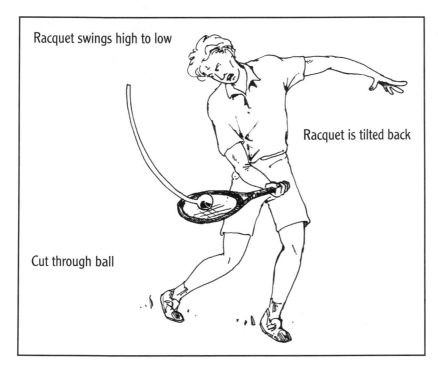

Racquet swings high to low

Racquet is tilted back

Cut through ball

FIGURE 21.5 Backspin.

SINGLES SCORING			
Skill	**Cue**	**Alternate Cue**	**Common Error**
Rules	Love (0), 15, 30, 40, game		
	15–0 = 15–love 0–15 = love–15	First score is the server's score In this game love means nothing	Saying receiver's score first
	30–30 = 30 all		
	40–40 = deuce	Win by two, deuce and ad	
	Scoring is used for game, set, and match		
	Ad in: server's advantage		
	Ad out: opponent's advantage		
	Or in "no ad": 1–2–3–game		
	No ad after 3–3		
	Next point is game point		
	Receiver chooses side on which to receive serve		
Playing a Set	Change sides on the odd-numbered games: 1, 3, 5, 7		
	Win 6 games; win by 2 games		
	If each player wins 6 games, a tiebreaker is played		
Match Play	Win 2 out of 3 sets, women		
	Win 3 out of 5 sets, men	Only in certain tournaments	

DOUBLES SCORING			
Skill	**Cue**	**Alternate Cue**	**Common Error**
Rules	Partner A1 serves one complete game	After the set you can serve two in a row (at the end of first set and beginning of second set the server can serve two)	
	Partners always serve from opposite sides of court		
	Opponent B1 serves one complete game		
	Partner A2 serves one complete game		
	Opponent B2 serves one complete game		
Doubles Receiver	Beginning of set, each player chooses which side to receive— deuce or ad court	Deuce court = right side Ad court = left side	Switching during set
	Must stay in that court to receive serve		Receiver's teammate stepping into server's box
	Change sides of court every odd game		

Chapter 22

Track and Field Events

INTRODUCTION

How can I go over the hurdle faster? How do I improve my sprint time? What's the best way to exchange the baton? Students and athletes might ask you questions such as these. Are you ready to answer without giving them too much technical information?

An effective way to teach track and field skills is to provide teaching cues. Teaching cues are simple and to the point. Good visual teaching cues help athletes create visual images for better concentration and consequently help to perfect techniques.

For example, when teaching the use of starting blocks, have students make a check mark with their hands at the starting line. The check mark cues the student to establish the correct hand position. Another example: when teaching the long jump, feedback from the coach might include "Mark, I really liked how you arched your back like a C in the air; however, make sure you close the jackknife on your landing a little sooner."

Giving students or athletes visual teaching cues can make a significant difference in the outcome of a race or event. A tenth of a second faster time or an inch difference in a throw or jump could mean advancing to regionals and then state competition.

SKILLS LISTED WITH CUES

Teaching cues in this chapter include the following: starting blocks, sprinting form, turns, relays, hurdles, steeplechase, distance running and jumping events (long jump, triple jump, high jump), and throwing events (shot put and discus).

Each event is broken down into its component phases, and cues are provided for each phase of the skill. The cues can be used in teaching the beginner or in helping the experienced athlete perfect his or her technique.

TIPS

When using a four-station rotation system for a large class, do not include more than one dangerous event. (For example, do not include both shot put and high jump.) The four stations might include starts, shot put (a dangerous station where the teacher should be present), distance runs, and long jump.

EQUIPMENT TIPS FOR RUNNING EVENTS

1. Starts: Blow a whistle to replace gun; use toilet paper for finish line.
2. Use large orange cones, dowel sticks, PVC pipe, or bamboo poles to make hurdles, or use foam rubber practice hurdles. Students are less likely to get hurt because foam hurdles are light in weight (see Figure 22.1).

EQUIPMENT TIPS FOR JUMPING EVENTS

1. High jump: Use elastic surgical tubing as a crossbar (see Figure 22.1).
2. Use grass for long jumps and triple jumps for large classes (see Figure 22.2).

EQUIPMENT TIPS FOR THROWING EVENTS

1. Use lightweight safe substitutes for competitive implements. If you don't have enough equipment, introduce the event as a station activity.
2. Shot put: Use tennis balls filled with lead shot and bound in tape or soft softballs.
3. Discus: Use rubber rings, small hula hoops.
4. Javelin: Use balls.

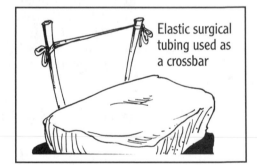

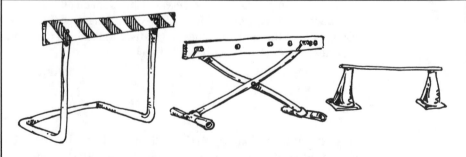

Modified hurdles may include cones, dowel sticks, PVC pipe, and pieces of wood with holes

FIGURE 22.1   Equipment Ideas for a Track and Field Unit.

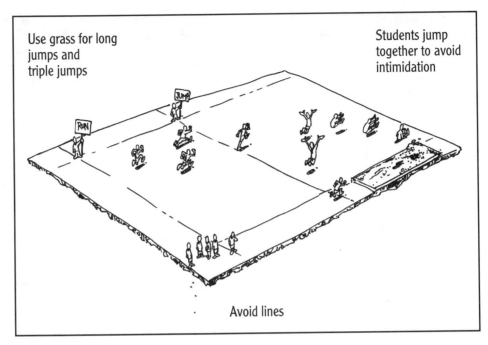

Use grass for long jumps and triple jumps

Students jump together to avoid intimidation

Avoid lines

FIGURE 22.2 Teaching Long Jump to a Physical Education Class.

TEACHING IDEAS

1. Have all students practice long jump and triple jump together, shoulder to shoulder on the grass instead of one at a time in the pit, until they gain some proficiency in the sport. Everyone will get more practice, and students may be less self-conscious than they might be jumping in front of their peers.

2. Teaching progression: Teach shot put first, and discus second. Use modified equipment for large classes or beginners as described under "Equipment Tips."

FYI

For further information and special help, consult the following organization and source:

USA Track and Field
One Hoosier Dome, Suite 140
Indianapolis, IN 46225
Phone: (317) 261–0500

Carr, G. (1991). *Fundamentals of track and field.* Champaign, IL: Leisure Press.

STARTING BLOCKS

Skill	Cue	Alternate Cue	Common Error
"On Your Marks"	Back into blocks		No routine, no order, no sequence
	Front foot goes in first, back foot second		
	Hands make a check mark (behind starting line) (Figure 22.3)	Thumb and forefinger behind line	Weight on thumb and knuckles
	Shoulders over hands	Weight forward	Weight back, shoulders behind hands
	Eyes looking down	Head is level	Dropping the head
	Sit in blocks		
"Set"	Buttocks up	Come up in one quick motion	Coming up too slow, buttocks lower than the head
	Lean until you are just about ready to fall	Chest over line	Sitting in the blocks
	Body still like statue		Moving body

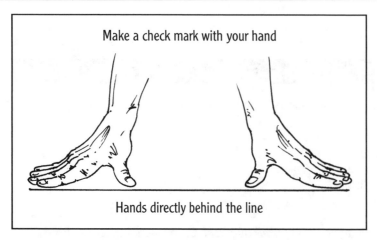

Make a check mark with your hand

Hands directly behind the line

FIGURE 22.3   Hand Position for the Sprint Starts.

STARTING BLOCKS

Skill	Cue	Alternate Cue	Common Error
"Gun"	Drive opposites (right arm, left leg or left arm, right leg)	Punch hand to ear (answer the telephone)	Right arm and right leg come out of blocks first or left arm and left leg
	Back leg drives out of block	Back foot steps straight ahead	Stepping with forward leg first
	Explode out of the blocks at 45-degree angle	Like a lunge position	Standing straight up
	Short, quick steps	Feet contact track directly under hip	

SPRINTING—50, 100, 200, 400 METERS

Skill	Cue	Alternate Cue	Common Error
Racing Form (Figure 22.4)			
Hip–Torso Action	Tall	As if someone is picking you up by the hair	Too much forward lean
	Tummy flat	Make a pillar with the hips and torso	
	Buttocks tucked under		

Run tall, as if someone is picking you up by the hair

Hammer nails in wall behind you

Hammer nails

Snap leg down

Pawing action

FIGURE 22.4   Sprinter.

SPRINTING—50, 100, 200, 400 METERS

Skill	Cue	Alternate Cue	Common Error
Racing Form (cont.)			
Arm Action	Hammer and nails	Pump the arms	Arms crossing midline of body
	Hammer nails in wall behind you	Hands to shoulder	
Hand Position	Hold a newspaper	Thumb in pocket	Fists clenched
	Hold a penny	Thumb rests on forefinger	Floppy hands
Leg Action	Heel to buttocks	Kick buttocks	Not enough knee flexion
	Step over opposite knee	Thigh parallel to ground	Knee lift too low
	Toe to knee	Point toe to sky	Pointing toe to ground before contact
	Snap leg down	Extend, reverse lower leg	Not snapping leg down
	Ground contact with ball of foot		Stopping foot on contact with ground

TURNS

Skill	Cue	Alternate Cue	Common Error
Body Position	Lean into curve	Look over a cliff	Standing tall in curve
Position of Feet in Curve	Rotate feet slightly in	Put right foot in door to stop from closing	Feet turn outward
Right Arm in Curve	Right arm crosses midline slightly	Pump right elbow slightly toward outside of track	Arm does not cross midline of body
Left Arm in Curve	Left arm normal	Hammer and nails	Left arm crosses midline in front
			Left elbow crosses elbow in back
Straightaway	Both arms return to normal sprint action at straightaway	Hammer and nails	Arms still cross midline of the body

RELAYS—BLIND HANDOFF UNDERHAND

Skill	Cue	Alternate Cue	Common Error
Receiver Arm Position	Slam the door directly behind you	Thumb in toward backbone; make a check mark toward ground	Arm extended outward
Hand Position	Steady hand	Make a target	Hand and arm moving
Passer Arm Position	Hit the palm with under-handed delivery	Focus eyes on hand; hit target	Trying to pass before target appears
Passer's Code	"Go" or other cue	One-syllable cue	Not loud enough Yelling at wrong time
Exchange	Receiver and passer should be at full speed when exchange takes place	Passer yells, "Hit"	Passer is too fast Receiver not at full speed

RELAYS—VISUAL HANDOFF

Skill	Cue	Alternate Cue	Common Error
Receiver	Turn head back toward passer, judge incoming runner's speed		Taking off too soon or too late
	Take two accelerating steps, then turn		
	Point hand at incoming runner	Palm up, elbow down	
	Take the baton from incoming runner	Take the money and run	Dropping the money (baton)
	Steady hand		
Passer	Hold the baton up when receiver turns	Fully extended arm at shoulder level	Watching other competitors
	Full speed until receiver has baton	Run through pass	Slowing before pass

RELAYS—BLIND HANDOFF OVERHAND (MORE COMPLEX)

Skill	Cue	Alternate Cue	Common Error
Receiver's Arm and Hand Position	Arm and hand parallel to ground		Hand bent up at wrist
	Palm up, elbow up	Thumb points at incoming runner	Arm and hand too low
Passer's Arm Position	Punch baton into target	Piston-type motion	Passing the baton from above shoulders coming down
			Passing baton before target appears
	Focus eyes on hand		Eyes wandering
Passer's Code	"Go" or other cue	One-syllable word	Not loud enough
			Yelling at wrong time
Exchange	See target before pass	Passer yells, "Hit"	Passer is too fast, receiver not at full speed

LOW HURDLES

Skill	Cue	Alternate Cue	Common Error
Body Position			
Before Hurdles	Short last step	Pawing action (like a horse)	Sitting, planting drive leg in front of hip
Over Hurdles	Exaggerated sprinting form over the hurdles	Run over the hurdles	Jumping over hurdles
Between Hurdles	Sprinting form between hurdles	Heel to butt, toe to knee	Last step before hurdle is too long
		Thigh parallel to ground	
		Body erect	
Lead Arm (Figure 22.5)	Reach toward opposite knee	Half jackknife position	Crossing midline of body too far
	Drive elbow back quickly	Like a karate punch	

Drive elbow back

Reach toward opposite knee

Half jackknife

Extend leg like a switchblade

FIGURE 22.5 Going Over Low Hurdle.

LOW HURDLES

Skill	Cue	Alternate Cue	Common Error
Trail Arm	Drive elbow back		
Lead Leg (Figure 22.5)	Upper leg flexed	Heel to buttocks	Straight lead leg
	Extend like a switchblade		
	Snap foot downward and backward	Vigorous pawing action	Toe contact too far forward of hips
	Ball of foot lands under hip		
Trail Leg	Hips parallel to hurdle	Draw half moon	Hips not parallel
	Lead with knee		Lead with thigh
	Toes averted	Foot flexed	Toes pointed down
	Snap foot down "quick"		
Equal and Opposite Reaction	Half jackknife position over hurdle, then tall position when foot touches ground	Open switchblade	Getting tall too soon or too late

STEEPLECHASE

Skill	Cue	Alternate Cue	Common Error
Water Jump	Stay short	Keep center of gravity close to hurdle	Standing tall
			Arms flapping around
	Lean forward		Slowing down before the hurdle
	Push off the back of the hurdle		Stepping on top of hurdle
Stationary Barriers	Same as 400 hurdle		
	Lean forward	Stay as low as possible	
	Accelerate into the hurdle	Keep up speed	
	Be conscious of trail leg	The barrier does not move	

DISTANCE RUNNING

Skill	Cue	Alternate Cue	Common Error
Body Position	Relax the face, neck, shoulders, and arms	Body erect	Face, neck, shoulders, and arms are tense/ tight
Hand Position	Thumb rests on the index finger, as if reading a newspaper	Hold a teacup	Clenched fist or floppy hands
Arm Position	Arms swing forward and back	Arms brushing hips	Arms cross midline of the body—high arm swing
Leg Position	Use shorter steps than sprinting		Bouncing up and down
			Long stride

DISTANCE RUNNING

Skill	Cue	Alternate Cue	Common Error
Foot Position	Strike heel and roll to toe	As if pushing on gas pedal	Striking toes first
	Toes straight ahead or slightly out		Feet are pigeon-toed
Head Position	Head straight ahead	Eyes focused straight ahead	Head down or up
Breathing	Breathe from the stomach (avoid side aches)	As if taking a breath to play a musical instrument	Breathing from chest
Thought Process	Think positive thoughts	"I feel great" "I am strong" "Body is moving well"	

LONG JUMP

Skill	Cue	Alternate Cue	Common Error
Approach	Start with takeoff foot	Same foot forward as jump-off foot	Changing starting/ jumping foot
	12 to 18 strides	Younger athletes, fewer strides	Too many strides
		Faster athletes, more strides	
	Accelerate to maximum usable speed	Same approach every time	Changing speed of the approach
	Knees up and tall in last strides	As if someone is lifting you by the hair	

LONG JUMP

Skill	Cue	Alternate Cue	Common Error
Takeoff	Last two steps, like a layup in basketball	Last two steps: long-short	Last step too long
	Jump up and out		
	Drive up knee and opposite arm vigorously	Overemphasize knee lift and arm drive	Not driving up free knee and opposite arm
Action in the Air (Figure 22.6)	Body makes a curve, like a half moon	Arch back like a C	Upper body ahead of hips
		Knees and feet behind hips	
	Arms above head and behind shoulders		
	Close jackknife	Extend legs and throw arms past knees	Little or no leg action
			Arms are not thrown past knees
Landing	Collapse buttocks to heels upon landing	Collapse at knees	Straight-leg landing on buttocks
	Arms thrust forward		
	Feet together		Feet apart

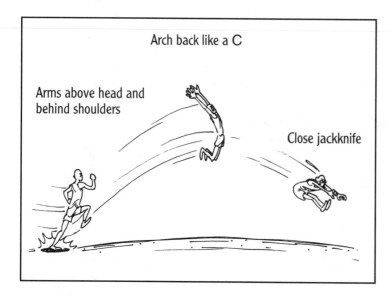

FIGURE 22.6 Long Jump.

TRIPLE JUMP			
Skill	**Cue**	**Alternate Cue**	**Common Error**
Approach	Start with jumping foot forward		Changing starting/ jumping foot (takeoff foot)
	12 to 18 strides	Younger athletes fewer strides	
		Faster athletes more strides	
	Knees up and tall in last five or six strides	As if someone is lifting you up by the hair	Overstriding or sitting
	Maximum speed	Same approach every time	Last step too long
	Last two steps like a layup in basketball	Long-short last two steps	Landing on opposite foot
Hop	Take off and land on same foot	Like hopscotch	Landing on opposite foot
	Tall upper body	As if you're wearing a back brace	Leaning forward at waist
	Head and eyes level	Look ahead	Looking down at ground, head down
	Knee up, toe up	Knee and toe flexed	Straight leg
	Snappy, pawing action	Active landing	No pawing action
			Leg does not snap down
Step	Long step, as if stepping over mud puddles	Take off and land on opposite foot	Hopping again
	Tall upper body	As if you're wearing a back brace	Leaning forward at waist
	Head and eyes level	Look ahead	Looking down at the ground, head down
	Split in air	Wide thigh separation during step	Short steps
	Landing—snappy, pawing action	Active landing	No pawing action

TRIPLE JUMP			
Skill	**Cue**	**Alternate Cue**	**Common Error**
Jump			
Arm Action	Reach for the sky	Drive arms upward	Not driving arms upward
Head and Eye Position	Head and eyes level	Look ahead	Looking down
Body Action	Close jackknife	Extend legs from hips	No hips
	Throw arms past knees	As if driving ski poles back at the start of the race	Reaching hands to feet
	Collapse buttocks to heels upon landing		Straight-leg landing on buttocks
Ground Contact	Even cadence throughout jump	Even rhythm	Uneven cadence
		Feet make "ta ta ta" sound: "even-even-even step"	Feet make "taaa ta ta" sound: "long-short-short step"

HIGH JUMP			
Skill	**Cue**	**Alternate Cue**	**Common Error**
Approach	Start even with standards	One foot outside standards	
Running Stride	Make a J	Half circle	Running straight at the bar
	The last four steps start the turn for the J	Get speed in run first	
Body Position	Lean into curve	Body weight inside of curve	Standing tall in curve
Running Stride	Last three steps medium, long, short		Last three steps too long or short

HIGH JUMP

Skill	Cue	Alternate Cue	Common Error
Takeoff			
Legs	Foot placed parallel to bar	Take off from outside foot	Inside foot used to take off
	Takeoff foot down quickly, as if stepping on a bug	Plant power leg, active landing	Take off with both feet
			Failing to plant power leg, no power in run or jump
	Drive the lead knee vigorously up		Not driving knee up
Arms	"Double arm gather" (use both arms behind the head like a slam dunk)	"Dunk it" Reverse slam dunk	Using legs only
Flight			
Body Position	Arch like a banana	"Golden arches"	Flat back
Arm Position	"See two fists"	See both hands up next to eyes after doing arm gather	Hands not visible Dropping fists

SHOT PUT

Skill	Cue	Alternate Cue	Common Error
Enter/Exit Position	Enter ring from rear	Exit from rear	Entering and exiting ring from side or front
Hold Shot	Wrap four fingers firmly around shot (Cradle Shot)	Hold shot on finger pads	Dropping the elbow and having the shot roll into palm
	Keep shot firm against neck		

SHOT PUT

Skill	Cue	Alternate Cue	Common Error
Release of Shot	Push shot through head	Shot leaves from neck, a "put" not a throw	Throwing like a baseball
	Punch at a 7-foot giant	Release is fast like a punch and at a 45-degree angle	Punch is horizontal
		Reach for stars	
Start of Glide	Think position facing back toward direction of throw	Focus in back of ring	Hurring start and keeping weight back
	Hips like a baseball swing	Hips open up quick like a baseball swing	Trying to throw before reaching power position
	Kick backward with nonsupport leg		
Explosion of Glide	Block–push–shoot (left leg straightens hard, right leg pushes up and out, causing a "shooting motion")	Keep shot back last	Legs collapse on thrower
End of Throw	Slap and pull		

DISCUS			
Skill	**Cue**	**Alternate Cue**	**Common Error**
Enter/Exit	Enter ring from back	Exit ring from back	Entering and exiting ring from rear
Holding the Discus	Open-handed eagle-claw grip	Carry a textbook Relax fingertips on edge of discus	Letting discus fall from hand Not gripping solidly
Release	Discus leaves off index finger as if releasing a bowling ball	Bowl the discus	Holding on to discus too long
The Wind	Twist and shout Keep body wound up until throw, then shout	Shout makes discus go farther	Only half winding
Explosion of Throw	Hips lead like a baseball swing	Hips open quick like a baseball swing	Throwing before reaching power position
End of Throw	Long pull (smooth like a golf swing) Head and chest up facing sector Block–push–shoot		Hurrying the throw release (will cause discus to flutter like a dead duck) Legs collapse

Chapter 23

Tumbling

INTRODUCTION

Tumbling is the most popular event in gymnastics because not much equipment is required for it. All that is needed is a flat surface area—a lawn, a living room, a football field, a basketball floor, a trampoline. Tumbling can be done anywhere and everywhere.

Tumbling is a sport that combines flexibility, strength, and coordination. Tumbling is for all ages. There is something exciting and intriguing about the body in motion. The wonder of the sport is the skills and movements that defy the limits placed on us by gravity.

SKILLS LISTED WITH CUES

Included in this chapter are simple cues to help instructors teach the following skills more efficiently: forward roll, front roll straddle, backward roll, backward roll straddle, handstand, back extension roll, cartwheel, front limber, pike dive roll, back handspring, and round off.

TIPS

1. Students should not be forced to do any tumbling skills. Ninety percent of injuries occur when they try to perform skills they are not ready to do on their own, often causing students to "chicken out."
2. The student should be completely confident before performing a skill. If a student is fearful or has had a bad experience, let the student choose which skill he or she would like to perform.
3. The most basic position is the handstand position. If a student can perform a good handstand, then she or he should be able to learn the more difficult skills involved in tumbling.

EQUIPMENT TIPS

1. Mats must be firm, padded, nonslippery, and clean.
2. Have students take shoes and socks off. Socks tend to make the skills more difficult by making contact with the mat difficult, and may cause one to slip.

3. There is a wide variety of tumbling surfaces available: spring tumbling floor, tumble tramp, ski tumble floor, and rod tumbling floor, to name a few.

TEACHING IDEAS

1. Flexibility and muscle-warming exercise are essential before practicing skills. Some suggested flexibility exercises for tumbling might include butterfly sit (two sets of 10 seconds), pike sit (hold for 30 seconds), straddle sit (hold each side for 30 seconds to 1 minute), and back bends (three sets, hold for 30 seconds to 1 minute). Also stretch wrists, ankles, shoulders, and neck.
2. Safety is a major concern for those who teach tumbling. The purpose of spotting is to aid students in practicing a skill safely and to prevent possible injury caused by landing incorrectly. The following list presents four safety and spotting suggestions:
    a. Know what the student is going to perform.
    b. Identify likely mishaps, and know when they might occur.
    c. Know what to spot and when the spot must occur.
    d. Have enough strength to assist if needed.
3. Once a student can confidently perform a single skill, other skills can be added to it. This progression can be followed with all tumbling skills. For example, the forward roll progression is as follows:
    a. Forward roll, stretch up
    b. Forward roll, tuck jump
    c. Forward roll, jump, half turn
    d. Forward roll, jump, full twist
    e. Forward roll, jump, straddle toe touch
    Students can perform more advanced skills once they feel comfortable performing a forward/backward roll and handstand (Masser, 1993). These skills help students improve their balance, coordination, and form when finishing a skill.
4. Have students design a routine with five to eight skills they feel comfortable performing.

FYI

For further information and special help, consult the following organization and source:

USA Gymnastics
Pan American Plaza, Suite 300
201 South Capital Avenue
Indianapolis, IN 46225
Phone: (317) 237–5050
Fax: (317) 237–5069

Weiss, M., Ebbeck, V., & Rose, D. (1992). "Show and tell" in the gymnasium revisited: Developmental differences in modeling and verbal rehearsal effects on motor skill learning and performance. *Research Quarterly for Exercise and Sport, 63*(3), 292–301.

BASIC STARTING POSITIONS AND RULES

Skill	Cue	Alternate Cue	Common Error
Basic Start Position	Ankles together, stand tall, arms reach toward ceiling		Legs apart, slumping Elbows bent
Lunge Position	Lunge position arms reach for ceiling	Front leg bent slightly, rear leg straight	
Rules	Tumble longer than your body		
	Wherever hands go, body follows		
	For every action, there is an equal and opposite reaction	As if body is a teeter-totter	
	Finish tall, reach for ceiling		

FORWARD ROLL

Skill	Cue	Alternate Cue	Common Error
Technique	Hips above head		
	Hands close to feet	Put hands flat on mat	Hands away from feet Not rounding back
	Forehead on knees	Look at chest	Pushing off ground one foot at a time
	Push off both feet and roll	As if feet are tied together and cannot come apart	Pushing into headstand instead of rolling forward
	Lower back down to mat using arms	Feel back stretching	Putting knees down on mat/rollover open
	Stand tall, reaching for ceiling	Squeeze stomach in, as if squeezing an orange	Standing up using knees instead of feet

FRONT ROLL STRADDLE

Skill	Cue	Alternate Cue	Common Error
Technique	Legs apart, knees locked in straddle position		Knees bent
	Put hands flat on mat		
	Head down, tuck chin, round back	Look at chest or belly button	Head up
	Push evenly off both feet and roll		Pushing with one foot
	Hands push hard between legs		Hands out to side, bending and unlocking knees
	Move shoulders forward quickly and forcefully		
	Stand tall, arms reach for ceiling		

BACKWARD ROLL

Skill	Cue	Alternate Cue	Common Error
Technique	Forehead on knees with hands on shoulders, palms up	Put hands on mat next to ears, push with hands, as if you are smashing something on ground next to ears	Head comes up as backward motion is started Not pushing evenly with hands when rolling over head
	Push off feet evenly	As if feet are tied together and cannot come apart	
	Roll back fast keeping forehead on knees	Knees glued to chest	Knees go up above head rather than past head
	Keep feet moving backward to find mat		
	When palms touch mat, push to force knees over and past head		Hands do not push off mat
	Stand tall		Landing with knees on mat instead of feet
	Reach for ceiling		

BACKWARD ROLL STRADDLE

Skill	Cue	Alternate Cue	Common Error
Technique	Legs apart, knees locked in straddle position		
	Bend forward		
	Place hands between legs and behind buttocks		
	Tuck chin, round back		
	Lean and roll quickly placing hands on mat beside ears		Not making quick transition of hands between legs to beside ears
	Push hard with hands, moving feet in straddle position to find mat	Move feet, find mat	Not pushing evenly with hands when rolling over head
	Stand tall, reach for ceiling, legs in straddle position		

HANDSTAND

Skill	Cue	Alternate Cue	Common Error
Hands Starting on Mat			
Ready Position	Dominant leg back, hands on mat		Shoulder over the heel of hand
	Shoulder over knuckles	Feel knuckles pushing into mat	
	Swing dominant leg up, lift other leg up to meet it		Switching legs in air
	Bring nondominant leg back down close to hands		Lifting leg when swinging leg up
	Keep head still throughout		Dropping head once legs are up

HANDSTAND			
Skill	**Cue**	**Alternate Cue**	**Common Error**
Standing			
Ready Position	Lunge position, reach for ceiling		
Motion	Kick rear leg forcefully upward and backward with body stretched	As if body is a teeter-totter	Body too loose
	Legs come together upside down, squeeze stomach, legs tight, knees locked	Touch toes to ceiling	Bending arms
	Push through shoulders to maintain handstand position		
	Step one leg down at a time to lunge position, arms reach toward ceiling		
Forward Roll from Handstand	Do a lunge and kick to handstand		Missing handstand, doing a forward roll
	Bend arms	Drop down and roll	Not bending arms, falling on back, or falling flat on back, like timber
	Tuck head		Not tucking
	Bring knees to chest		
	Back rounded		
	Roll forward, stand tall, arms reach for ceiling		

BACK EXTENSION ROLL			
Skill	**Cue**	**Alternate Cue**	**Common Error**
Technique	Bend knees with ankles together and begin a backward roll Forcefully extend hips, knees, and arms (to achieve vertical handstand position) Step down one leg at a time to lunge position Arms reach for ceiling	Touch toes to ceiling	Not extending hips, knees, and arms at correct time to achieve handstand

CARTWHEEL (RIGHT)			
Skill	**Cue**	**Alternate Cue**	**Common Error**
Technique (Figure 23.1)	Stand sideways with legs shoulder-width apart, arms reaching for ceiling Step with right foot to side and do a sideways lunge		Not keeping arms over head

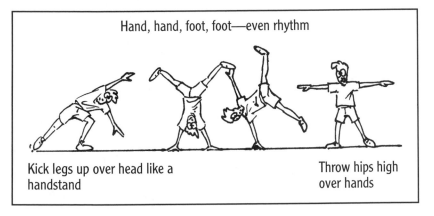

Hand, hand, foot, foot—even rhythm

Kick legs up over head like a handstand

Throw hips high over hands

FIGURE 23.1 Cartwheel.

CARTWHEEL (RIGHT)

Skill	Cue	Alternate Cue	Common Error
Technique *(cont.)*	Place right hand, then left hand on mat, while kicking left leg up and over head, with right leg following	Rhythm of hand, hand, foot, foot (1, 2, 3, 4, even rhythm)	Arms and legs collapse
	Throw hips high over hands		Hips not high enough
	Bring first foot down close to hands		Feet landing away from hands
	Land left leg then right leg, body remaining sideways throughout; end sideways	Stretch body through vertical	Not passing through vertical
			Bending at the hips
	Hands reaching toward ceiling		

FRONT LIMBER

Skill	Cue	Alternate Cue	Common Error
Technique	Do a lunge and kick to handstand		
	Push shoulders forward and let feet fall to a backbend position	Shoulders push toward wall they are looking at	Not landing on feet in backbend position
	Push hips forward, head back, arms up as weight is transferred from hands to feet	Hips forward Arms up Head back	Pulling head up too soon, dropping hips and arms, landing flat on back
	Look at person behind you	Rock back and forth from hands to feet to stand	
	Finish by reaching hands toward ceiling		
	Stand tall		

PIKE DIVE ROLL

Skill	Cue	Alternate Cue	Common Error
Technique (Figure 23.2)	Jump from both feet, ankles together, with arms directly over head	As if jumping over something high or jumping into forward roll	Not achieving a dive when jumping into the roll
	Legs straight, bend at hips	Get heels off floor fast	Not tucking head
	Hands land on mat, then tuck head, bend knees, and roll		
	Finish standing tall, arms reaching for sky		

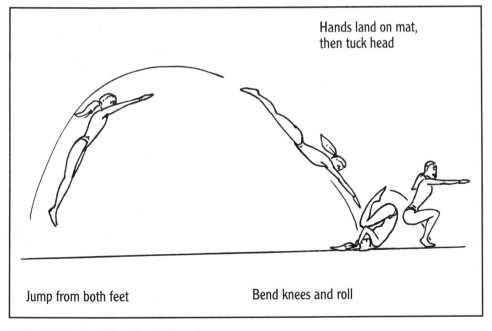

Hands land on mat, then tuck head

Jump from both feet

Bend knees and roll

FIGURE 23.2 Pike Dive Roll.

BACK HANDSPRING

Skill	Cue	Alternate Cue	Common Error
Technique	Arms above head, ankles together		
	Bend knees and swing arms straight forward and down by sides	Like sitting in a chair; chest remains upright	Leaning too far forward or backward
	Spring backward, swinging arms up while jumping		Not synchronizing arm swing with jump
	Look backward at hands while landing vertical in hand-stand position		Not looking at hands while jumping
	Push off hands to snap feet down, landing with arms up		Not landing on both feet

ROUND OFF (RIGHT)		
Skill	**Cue**	**Common Error**
Technique (Figure 23.3)	Begin in lunge position, right leg forward Hands go on mat as in cartwheel (1, 2) Kick left leg over head with right leg meeting left leg in vertical Quickly push off hands and snap feet together on mat Finish standing tall, arms reaching for sky	Feet are not together at top in vertical Pushing off hands slowly

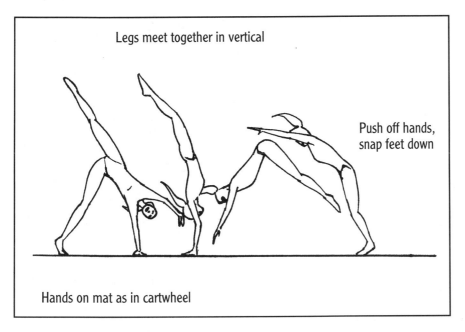

Legs meet together in vertical

Push off hands, snap feet down

Hands on mat as in cartwheel

FIGURE 23.3   Round Off.

Chapter 24

Ultimate Frisbee

INTRODUCTION

Ultimate Frisbee originated in Maplewood, New Jersey in 1968. It uniquely combines high competition with spirit of the game. "Spirit of the game" means no referees, honest playing, and positive spirits on and off the field. "Spirit" means ultimate athletes need not waste time faking out officials. Instead, efforts focus on high performance and going all out. Combining skills from sports ranging from soccer and Frisbee to basketball, ultimate Frisbee is a fast-paced, highly energetic noncontact sport that isn't for the lazy or pessimistic. In all other sports players are allowed to do anything until an official informs them that an activity is illegal. (In basketball it isn't a foul unless it is called as such.)

SKILLS LISTED WITH CUES

The cues in this chapter include the following skills: backhand throw, pull (full throw), forehand throw (sidearm), sandwich catching, offensive movement, and defensive marking.

TIPS

1. A certain level of maturity, trust, and honesty are required for the spirit of the game.
2. Seven players per team.
   a. Handlers (three players) are the first players to take a "pull" (similar to the kick-off in football). Generally these players are the most accurate throwers of the seven players on the field.
   b. Mids (two players) are players who generally have good cutting and maneuvering skills. They provide constant "flow" of the disk downfield with back or side cuts.
   c. Longs (two players) are players who have the ability to run fast, long back cuts into the end zone or at least downfield. Longs should have field sense and accurate catching skills.
3. Sub out when players get tired; keep a "fresh crew." Only when one team scores can a substitution be made.
4. You can only stand one Frisbee width from the player with the disk, and you count stalling "one two . . . eight nine ten." If the thrower still has the disk after ten is announced by the marker, it then becomes a turnover, and the other team gains position of the disk.

EQUIPMENT TIPS

1. Frisbee (175 grams official weight).
2. Cleats preferred.
3. Cones, lines, or flags to mark end zones and boundaries.
4. Field dimensions: 40 yards wide, 70 yards long, with 25-yard-long end zones.

TEACHING IDEAS

1. Play to 21, victory margin 2 points. Informal games can be played to other point totals or for a certain time period.
2. The game is started by both teams standing on opposite end lines. The disk is thrown to the other team as a kickoff. Players move the Frisbee down the field by throwing it to one another. If the Frisbee hits the ground or goes out of bounds, the other team gains possession. Once a player catches the disk in the end zone, a point is scored and the opposing team must walk to the far goal line and await the pull or throw-off from the scoring team.
3. The game can be played with as few as four players to a team on any flat open space available that has a fairly well marked end zone.

FYI

For further information and special help, consult the following organization:

Ultimate Players Association
3595 East Fountain Blvd.
Suite J 2
Colorado Springs, CO 80910
Phone: 1–800–UPA–GetH

Items include the following:
1. Teaching materials
2. Videos
3. Disks
4. Publications
5. Rules
6. How to start teams or leagues
7. College starter kit
8. How to teach ultimate Frisbee

THROWING

Skill	Cue	Alternate Cue	Common Error
Backhand (Figure 24.1)			
Grip	Pinch Frisbee edge with thumb and forefinger		
Throw	Wipe table with back of hand	Release, like snapping a towel	Releasing with disk at too much of an angle
	Pivot, windup, step, snap, release	Point finger at target after follow-through	Using too much arm motion
	Step at target		
Pull (Full Throw—Same as Kickoff in Football)	Same as backhand except preparatory steps		Incorrect release angle
			Misreading wind

Pinch Frisbee edge with thumb and forefinger

Release, like snapping a towel

FIGURE 24.1 Backhand Grip and Throw.

THROWING			
Skill	**Cue**	**Alternate Cue**	**Common Error**
Forehand (Sidearm) (Figure 24.2)			
Grip	Middle finger is pivot finger	Roll off middle finger	Incorrect grip
Throw	Outside rim of disk lower than inside	Step same side	Too much arm motion
	Step (same side) to target, snap towel		Incorrect release angle will cause disk to dive into ground
	Elbow on hip—wrist snap		Throwing like a baseball

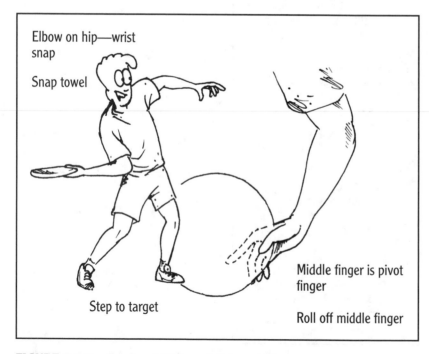

Elbow on hip—wrist snap

Snap towel

Step to target

Middle finger is pivot finger

Roll off middle finger

FIGURE 24.2   Forehand (Sidearm) Grip and Throw.

CATCHING

Skill	Cue	Alternate Cue	Common Error
Sandwich Catching	Watch Frisbee come to hands "Patty-cake" catch Clap before you catch	 Hands like a clam	Looking away, incorrect timing Not using both hands

OFFENSE

Skill	Cue	Alternate Cue	Common Error
Movement	Cut, circle away, cut, circle—keep moving! Fake and sharp cut Look while pivoting, fake, pivot, fake, anticipate! Lead teammate with throw	Lose defense Various speed doodling Throw to area, not to person, on long throw	Same speed movements "Banana" cut No faking movements Standing still Not giving player enough lead on throw

DEFENSE

Skill	Cue	Alternate Cue	Common Error
Marking (Figure 24.3)	Stick like glue Watch midsection	Play the unwanted little brother—opponent cannot get rid of you	Lack of conditioning Going for steal and losing opponent Watching head and feet—getting faked out Overrunning opponent

Stick like glue

Watch midsection

Play the unwanted little brother— opponent cannot get rid of you

FIGURE 24.3
Defensive Marking.

RULES			
Skill	**Cue**	**Alternate Cue**	**Common Error**
Basic Guidelines	The disk may never be handed—it must always be thrown		
	No player may move while in possession of the disk	Player may pivot on one foot in any direction, as in basketball	
	The disk may be thrown in any direction		
	No more than one player may guard a thrower	Use both legs and hands to guard or knock down the disk	Double guarding equals a free pass on the spot
	The defensive team gains possession of the disk whenever the offensive team's pass is incomplete, intercepted, knocked down, or goes out of bounds		

RULES			
Skill	**Cue**	**Alternate Cue**	**Common Error**
Basic Guidelines *(cont.)*	Out-of-bounds throws are taken over by the opposing team at the point where the disk went out of bounds No hand-slapping to knock the disk down or out of the hand of the passer If disk is passed to you, have three steps in which to stop	If a disk goes out of bounds after crossing goal line, opposing team may throw in from either corner of end zone at goal line No running with the disk	
Myths	Don't get a workout	Played with dogs	

Chapter 25

Volleyball

INTRODUCTION

Teachers and coaches face a monumental task when preparing instructional methods for teaching motor skills. They must make many decisions regarding content, method, class organization and control, evaluation, and methods of grading. When planning for content and method, one should be able to answer the following questions: Why did you teach that skill the way you did? Why was the instruction sequenced as it was? Why did the group practice like that? Why did you have them use instructional aids? Why did you say what you did to them?

Most, if not all, of these answers should be based on empirical evidence rather than on opinion, tradition, or the teacher's whim. Researchers have found that modeling facilitates motor-skill learning. Magill (1985) states, "Selecting the correct cues is one of the most important elements that an instructor includes in the teaching process."

In addition to focusing a student's attention on essential elements of the model, meaningful cues reduce the amount of information that is given. Because students attend to a limited amount of new material for a limited time, such a routine will enhance learning. For example, when teaching the block, the two cues are "Hands up" and "Make Mickey Mouse ears." These cues provide "hooks" on which to hang memories of the instruction. We find that our students can tell us many of the cues they received in their volleyball classes years later.

SKILLS LISTED WITH CUES

This chapter presents the cues for the following skills: ready position for forearm pass, forearm pass, overhead pass, setter's position and signals, serves (underhand and overhand), spiking, blocking, preparation for dig, forearm pass dig, dig (sprawl, pancake, overhead, fist), team strategies (offensive and defensive), and individual strategies (offensive and defensive).

The cues are listed in a recommended teaching sequence. A list of alternative cues is provided to benefit students who have difficulty linking the first cue with the desired performance. The alternate cues will suggest similar mental images that students may connect to more familiar motor patterns. Teachers should experiment with the cues and match the most helpful cue to each student's need.

TIP

1. After each drill have players perform a set number of push-ups and sit-ups. Strength gains happen very quickly, and time is utilized efficiently.

EQUIPMENT TIPS

1. Use a light ball to teach the basic skills (for example, a lightweight plastic ball found at most discount department stores).
2. Leather balls are better than rubber balls in preventing the arms from being hurt.
3. Lower the nets, or have students work back to the baseline on serving drills.
4. Use blackboard and chalk to record competitive drills and the like.

TEACHING IDEAS

1. When possible perform drills that contain the playing sequence—that is, "pass, set"; "serve, pass, set, hit"; "dig, set, hit"; and so on.
2. Drills should always have a specific goal (i.e., targets, scores, hit a certain number in a row perfectly, create competition with score 13–13, hit until you lose, etc).
3. Always end drills on a positive note.
4. Games take 20 to 40 minutes to play. Some drills need to be as long as game time.
5. If court space is available, play two-on-two, three-on-three, or four-on-four games.

FYI

For further information and special help, consult the following organizations:

Canyon Volleyball
c/o Carl McGown
3815 Riverwood Drive
Provo, UT 84604
Phone: (801) 225–9271
Fax: (801) 225–9273

Provides information about volleyball coaching clinics.

USA Volleyball
4510 Executive Drive, Plaza 1
San Diego, CA 92121–3009
Phone: (619) 625–8200
Fax: (619) 625–8212

U.S. Volleyball Association
3595 East Fountain Boulevard, Suite 1–2
Colorado Springs, CO 80910
Phone: (719) 637–8300
Fax: (719) 637–6307

PASSES			
Skill	**Cue**	**Alternate Cue**	**Common Error**
Forearm			
Ready Position	Hands on knees		Weight on heels instead of balls of feet
			Knees locked straight
Execution (Figure 25.1)	Wrists and hands together	Lifelines together	Elbows held at sides, arms too close to body
	Forearm contact with ball	Hide your chest	Hitting ball on wrists
	Fat part of arms hits ball		Hitting ball on wrists
	Elbows straight and simple	Make a flat surface with the forearms	Bending elbows, moving arms up and down to add power
	Face ball, angle arms	Pass over lead leg	Facing target
	Shuffle	Beat ball to the spot	
	See the server, see the ball		

See the server,
see the ball

Face ball,
angle arms

Pass over lead leg

FIGURE 25.1   Forearm Pass.

PASSES			
Skill	**Cue**	**Alternate Cue**	**Common Error**
Overhead (Figure 25.2)	Big hands	As if looking at the bottom of a full bowl of cereal	
Execution	Shape early	Hands up at hairline	
	Extend	Like a basketball chest pass, elbows straighten	Ball staying in contact with hands too long— violation
			Only using arms to push ball
	Face target	Over lead leg	Setting over right or left shoulder, sideways

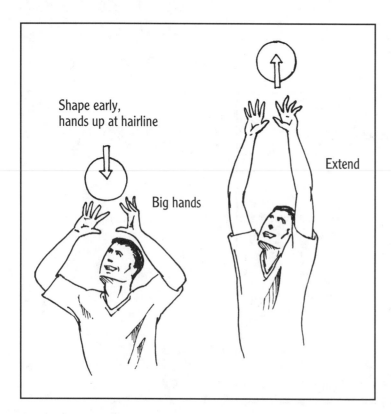

Shape early, hands up at hairline

Big hands

Extend

FIGURE 25.2 Overhead Pass.

SETTER'S POSITION

Skill	Cue	Alternate Cue	Common Error
Technique	Right shoulder to net		Not looking at pass early enough
	Stand next to or as close as possible to the net		Trying to pass a serve
	Right side of court, front row		
	Shape early		
	Extend		
	Face target		
Back Set	Hips forward	Extend back	
	See setter's signals		

SERVES

Skill	Cue	Alternate Cue	Common Error
Underhand			
Leg Action	Step toward net with foot opposite to throwing arm		Stepping forward with same leg as serving arm
Hand Position	Palm up, make a fist	Thumb rests on side of index finger	
	Arm close to body, brush shorts		
	Elbow straight		Elbow bent
	Hit ball out of hand		Tossing ball into air
	Like pitching horseshoes	Follow-through toward target	Arm action stops at ball contact
Overhead	Bow and arrow		
	Toss it (step, toss, hit)	Toss in front of serving shoulder	Rotating shoulder forward, elbow stays back
	Heel to target	Contact ball at top of toss	Hitting behind or on top of ball
	Have a routine you do each time	Like basketball free throw routines	

SPIKING			
Skill	**Cue**	**Alternate Cue**	**Common Error**
Execution (Figure 25.3)	Four-step approach: R–L–R–L if right-handed L–R–L–R if left-handed		No approach, starting approach too close to net
	Arms forward—back—forward	Hitting hand goes behind net	Jumping off only one leg like a basketball layup
	Bow and arrow action		
	Fingers apart	Hand open and firm	Fist
	Hand in shape of ball	Wrist somewhat stiff	Hand is flat, fist, or Jell-O
Timing	First step when ball is set	Stepping and setting Trust eyes; do not guess	Running too far forward; ball goes over attacker's head
	Contact ball high and in front of you		Contacting ball too low or behind head
	Fast arm swing	Powerful wrist snap	No wrist snap

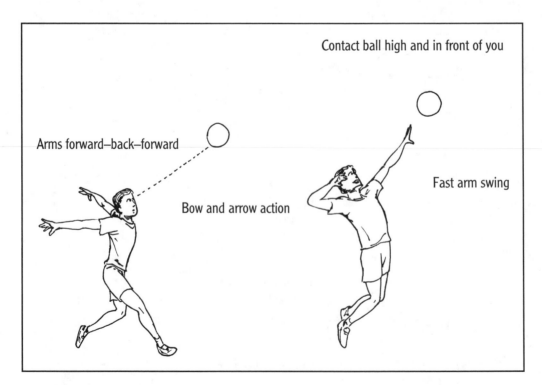

Contact ball high and in front of you

Arms forward–back–forward

Bow and arrow action

Fast arm swing

FIGURE 25.3   Spike.

BLOCKING

Skill	Cue	Alternate Cue	Common Error
Set-Up (Figure 25.4)	Keep hands up at eye level	Knees bent ready to jump	Bringing hands and arms below net, straight legs
	Seal the net with body	Chin down for peripheral vision	Body too far from net
Arm Action	Hands up as if playing a piano	Fingers are firm and spread—Mickey Mouse ears	Fingers close together and not firm
Timing	Ball, setter, ball, hitter	Lead step	Hands down at sides
			Watching nothing but the ball
	Three-step move	Get over	Moving with hands down at waist
	Penetrate	Angle hands into opponent's court as if diving into a swimming pool	Being too far away from net
	Reach over		

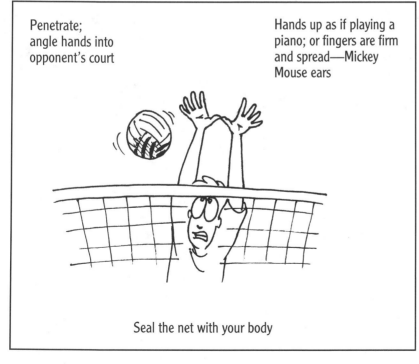

Penetrate; angle hands into opponent's court

Hands up as if playing a piano; or fingers are firm and spread—Mickey Mouse ears

Seal the net with your body

FIGURE 25.4   The Block.

DIGS			
Skill	**Cue**	**Alternate Cue**	**Common Error**
Preparation	Anticipate spike		
	Feet apart, arms ready		Weight back on heels, standing straight up
	Ball, setter, ball, hitter	Watch hitter's shoulders and head	Watching ball, not hitter
	Knees bent		
Forearm Pass	Arms like a wall	Don't swing arms	Swinging arms
	Absorb shock of spike	Like a sponge	
	Platform underneath ball		Arms too close to body
Sprawling	Anticipate spike	Be stopped when hitter contacts ball	Still moving when hitter contacts ball
	Big step	Close to floor, chin up	No tennis hop
	Hit ball, then sprawl	First things first	Falling over instead of moving feet
	Helping hand		
	Turn knee out		
Pancake	Big step	Close to floor	Not moving feet fast enough
	Helping hand		
	Turn knee out		
	Slide hand on floor		
Overhead	Tomahawk action		Contact between ball and hands is too long to be legal
	Deflection or rebound back toward net		
Fist	Flat surface		

SETTER'S SIGNALS			
Skill	**Cue**	**Alternate Cue**	**Common Error**
Setter	Quarterback of team—signals with fingers to spiker and team	Calls the set signal by using a hand signal to notify players of type of play	Other players call the signal
Height of Set; Spiker on the Court	4 3 3 2 ———— 1 ———— net 5 4 3 2 1 A B C Setter		

Spiker's Court Position to Net	Setter signals for first number or letter	Examples:
		  1–1 short set
		  5–1 long short set
			Not listening or looking for signal from setter

Height of Ball Number	Setter signals for second number	Examples:
		  5–4 high set
		  C–4 high back set
			Confusing the numbers

Short Sets *1–1, 3–1, A–1, C–1*	"You go, I throw" Spiker watches ball go over shoulder	Correct timing takes practice	Not watching ball, moving too late or too early
	As soon as ball passes shoulder, chase the ball to net	Stay with it	Becoming frustrated and quitting
Medium Sets *1–2, 3–2*	When the ball leaves setter's hands, go!		
High Sets *5–4, C–4*	"I throw, you go" Go when the ball leaves the setter's hands	Watch where ball is set	Leaving too soon Not watching the ball leave the setter's hands

SETTER'S HAND SIGNALS

Skill	Cue	Alternate Cue	Common Error
End of Play			
Setter's Responsibility	Setter gives signal before ball is served	Setter gives signal at side of leg to prevent opponent from seeing it	
Hitters' Responsibility	Hitters look for setter's signal as soon as play is over		Forgetting to look for setter's hand signals
	Move with setter on calls	Everybody watch pass, move accordingly	Not looking for setter's hand signals

net
‾‾‾‾‾‾‾‾‾
  S   S
  H   H

Skill	Cue	Alternate Cue	Common Error
During Rally			
Hitters' Responsibility	Hitters can call signals 1–5–C		
Front Sets	Thumb, index, and middle fingers used for front sets		
Short Set	Index finger = 1–1		
	Index and middle finger = 1–2		
Middle Front Set	Thumb, index, and middle finger = 3–2		
	Four fingers = 4–4		
Long Set	Five fingers = 5–4		
Back Sets	Pinkie and ring finger used for back sets		
Short Back Set	Pinkie finger = A1		
Middle Back Set	Pinkie finger and ring finger = B2		
High Back Set	Make letter C = C4		

TEAM STRATEGIES

Skill	Cue	Alternate Cue	Common Error
Offense	Stress passing and serving over all other skills		
	Use all three contacts if possible, or other team will		
	Only attempt technically what players can do physically; do not do too much		
	Setter is the most athletic player on team, most important		
	Sets must be high in order to attack		
	Talk to each other when passing, hitting, and so forth		
Defense	Funnel attack to back-row players	First do offense, then defense	
	Front-row players stay close to net		
	Stay low, with good center of gravity		
	Front-row attackers never reach back for a dig; someone will be punched in the face		

INDIVIDUAL STRATEGIES		
Skill	**Cue**	**Common Error**
Offense	Front-row hitters, stay away from net	
	When hitting, keep ball in front of you	
	Try to anticipate what will happen before it happens	
	Hit around the blockers, even if ball cannot be hit it as hard by doing it	
Defense	Be ready for anything, all the time	
	Weight on balls of feet, not heels	
	Try to anticipate attacks	
	If you intend to pass or dig a ball, call for it: "I go," "Mine"	
	Talk!	

Chapter 26

Weight Lifting (Strength Exercises)

INTRODUCTION

"In the early 1900s Alan Calvert developed adjustable barbells with weighted plates that could be added or removed to change the resistance. In more than 80 years few changes have altered his basic design" (Allsen, Harrison, & Vance, 1993).

Free weights have an advantage over machines in that they require the participant to balance the weights when lifting, using more muscles and training all muscle groups. When using free weights, the student progresses more quickly than when using machines. Many body builders prefer free weights.

To include weight lifting in the curriculum, teachers need to have the appropriate equipment and to be able to offer a weight-lifting program for at least six weeks (the time it takes for the body to adapt to the regimen). By using a different lift for the same muscle group the student can continue to progress.

SKILLS LISTED WITH CUES

We provide cues for the following free-weight lifts: squat, bench press, power snatch, and power clean, as well as safety guidelines. Also provided under "Teaching Ideas" are suggested regimens for a variety of push-ups, sit-ups, and dips.

TIPS

1. Each muscle group should be exercised three days a week.
2. Stretch before and after lifting.
3. Complete the full range of motion during any lift. Don't do partial or half movements.
4. Lifting weights should be a controlled movement. Avoid jerking movements. The positive move (concentric) is usually faster than the negative move (eccentric).
5. Push-ups (modified or regulation), sit-ups, abdominal curls, and dips are great strength exercises that can be done any time, any place (Figure 26.1).

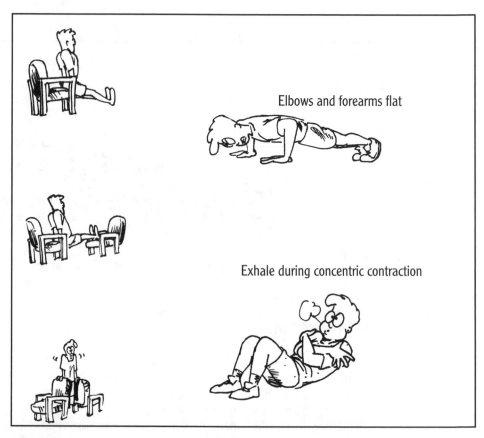

FIGURE 26.1   Push-Ups, Sit-Ups, and Dips Develop Rapid Strength Gains.

EQUIPMENT TIPS

1. Use two chairs or benches to perform modified dips.
2. Use mats, carpet squares, or grass to perform sit-ups and abdominal curls.
3. Body lifts: partner applies the resistance.
4. Boxes used for plyometric training: three boxes, 3-foot cubes; four boxes, 1-foot cubes.
5. Make weight-lifting belts available.

TEACHING IDEAS

1. Boxes used for plyometric training are great strength-building tools. Hurdles can also be used for plyometric training; adjust to specific height.
2. Have students chart their progress. Class or individual charts can be used. Students are motivated by seeing their progress.
3. Provide weight-lifting picture charts in weight rooms for students to refer to. These pictures can help teach correct weight-lifting techniques.
4. Always train with a partner, and train with one who has comparable strength. The partner spots the weight for the weight lifter. This method saves time because the lifter doesn't have to keep changing weights or taking weight off the bar.

5. Push-ups per day: Start with 10; work up to 50 to 300.
   a. Regulation.
   b. Modified with knees.
   c. Get on all fours and lift one hand or leg.
6. Push-up workout: Try three sets of five push-ups, working up to three sets of 10, 15, 20, 25.
7. Sit-ups work abdominal muscles. Sit-ups per day: Start with 10; work up to 50 to 300. Do sit-ups three to five days per week. Variations:
   a. Arms crossed in front.
   b. Arms behind neck.
   c. Arms at sides come up and touch toes.
   d. Crunches with legs up, bent; twist side to side.
   e. Rowing.
8. Sit-up workout: Try three sets of five sit-ups, working up to three sets of 10, 15, 20, 25.
9. Dips work shoulders, forearms, back of upper arms. Variations:
   a. Place palms on end of bench, feet on ground, and dip.
   b. Place palms on end of chair and feet on other chair, dip down.
   c. Use dip bars in weight room.
10. Dips workout: Dips take a little more strength. Start maybe with one set of 5 to 10 and work up to three sets of 15 to 20.
11. Try doing a set of push-ups, sit-ups, or dips by increasing the speed.
12. Rapid strength gains take place with lots of push-ups, sit-ups, and dips.

FYI

For further information and special help, consult the following organization:

National Strength & Conditioning
PO Box 81410
Lincoln, NE 68501
Phone: (402) 472–3000

SQUAT

Skill	Cue	Common Error
Abdominals	Abdominals held in tight	Being lazy
Stance	Feet shoulder-width apart, slightly pointed out	Feet parallel
	Knees soft, slightly back	Knees locked
Execution	Eyes at noon	Looking down or looking up too high (at the ceiling)
	Back straight and shoulders upright and tall	Rounding the back and bending over too much at the waist
	Weight on heels (water skier taking off or sitting down in chair)	Weight on toes with heels off ground
	Knees stay behind toes	Knees going beyond toes
	Upper thigh parallel to floor and knees at 90-degree angle	Going too low

BENCH PRESS

Skill	Cue	Common Error
Grip	Grip couple of inches wider than shoulder width	Too wide, too narrow
Feet Position	Feet flat on ground	
Back Position	Back flat on bench	Raising buttocks while lifting
Execution	Lightly touch chest when lowering bar	Bouncing bar off chest
	Lift should be smooth	If weight wobbles, too much weight
	Chest puffs out	Chest caves in
Incline Bench Press	Same as bench press except bring bar down to lightly touch collarbone	Bringing bar down too low
Decline Bench Press	Same as bench press except execution	
	Bring bar down to lightly touch the lower part of the chest	Bringing bar down too high on chest

POWER SNATCH

Skill	Cue	Common Error
Stance	Feet shoulder-width apart	Feet too wide
	Knees slightly bent	Knees too straight
	Bend at the waist so shoulders are in front of body	
	Tight back	Rounded back
Grip	Super wide grip (carrying a wide table by yourself)	
	Form wide V	
Execution	Drive with legs (jumping in the air)	Performing slowly
	Explode hips when bar reaches knees	
	Pull bar high with elbows high and close to body (like putting on your pants)	Bar away from body
	Drop under bar (hold world over head)	No drop
	Lock elbows and stand	Not locking elbows

POWER CLEAN

Skill	Cue	Common Error
Stance	Same as power snatch	
Grip	Just outside of knees	
Execution	Same as power snatch until catch	Elbows not getting high enough
	Rotate elbows under bar	Bar is away from body
	Drop body and catch bar on clavicle and front deltoids	

GENERAL RULES		
Skill	**Cue**	**Common Error**
Safety Guidelines (Figure 26.2)	Wear weight-lifting belt	
	Have spotter	
	Use collars	
	Control bar at all times	
	Inhale during eccentric contraction and exhale during concentric contraction	

FIGURE 26.2   Safety Guidelines.

References

Allsen, P. E., Harrison, J. M., & Vance, B. (1993). *Fitness for life. An individualized approach* (5th ed.). Madison, WI: WCB Brown Benchmark.

American Red Cross. (1992). *Swimming and diving*. St. Louis, MO: Mosby.

Blakemore, C. (1995). *Methods of designing cues*. Provo, UT: Brigham Young University.

Christiansen, R. (1995, August 22). [Cues for teaching]. Unpublished interview.

Christina, R. W., & Corcos, D. M. (1988). *Coaches guide to teaching sport skills*. Champaign, IL: Human Kinetics.

Darst, P. W., Zakrajsek, D. B., & Mancini, V. H. (1989). *Analyzing physical education and sport instruction*. Champaign, IL: Human Kinetics.

Docheff, D. M. (1990). The feedback sandwich. *Journal of Physical Education, Recreation and Dance, 64*, 17–18.

Fronske, H. (1993, May). Cueing beginning players in on good golf strokes. *Strategies, 6*(7), 25–29.

Fronske, H., Abendroth-Smith, J., & Blakemore, C. (in press). Critical overhand throwing cues help 3rd, 4th, and 5th grade students achieve efficient throwing patterns and increase their distance. *The Physical Educator*.

Fronske, H., & Birch, N. (1995). Overcoming road blocks to communication. *Strategies, 8*(8), 22–25.

Fronske, H., & Collier, C. (1993, September). Cueing your athletes on good jumping events. *Journal of Physical Education, Recreation and Dance, 64*(7), 7–9.

Fronske, H., Collier, C., & Orr, D. (1993, February). Cueing your participants in on track events. *Journal of Physical Education, Recreation and Dance, 64*(2), 9–10.

Fronske, H., & Dunn, S. (1992, February). Cue your students in on good swimming. *Strategies, 5*, 25–29.

Fronske, H., Dunn, S., & Wilson, R. (1992, May/June). Visual teaching cues for tennis instruction. *Journal of Physical Education, Recreation and Dance, 63*(5), 13–14.

Fronske, H., & McGown, C. (1992, October). Visual teaching cues for volleyball skills. *Journal of Physical Education, Recreation and Dance, 63*(8), 10–11.

Fronske, H., Schulz, A., & Searle, L. (1993, March). Cues you can use for fast pitch softball. *Scholastic Coach, 62*(8), 94–95.

Hall, L. T. (1994). *Motor learning lecture notes*. Dubuque, IA: Kendall/Hunt.

Harrison, J., & Blakemore, C. L. (1992). *Instructional strategies for secondary school physical education* (3rd ed.). Dubuque, IA: Wm. C. Brown.

Lawther, J. D. (1968). *The learning of physical skills.* Englewood Cliffs, NJ: Prentice-Hall.

Lockhart, A. (1966, May). Communicating with the learner. *Quest, VI,* 57–67.

Magill, R. (1985). *Motor learning: concepts and applications.* Dubuque, IA: Wm. C. Brown.

Masser, L. (1990, January). *Tchouk ball. An exciting coeducational game.* Paper presented at Share the Wealth Physical Education Conference, Jekyll Island, GA.

Masser, L. (1991, January). *Collaboration: what is needed.* Paper presented at the meeting of the National Association for Physical Education in Higher Education/AIESP, World Congress. Atlanta, GA.

Masser, L. (1993). Critical cues help first grade students' achievement in handstands and forward rolls. *Journal of Teaching in Physical Education, 12,* 301–312.

McGown, C. (1988). [Motor learning]. Unpublished lecture notes. Provo, UT: Brigham Young University.

Parker, D., & Bars, J. (1994). *On target for fun* [video]. Palm Beach, FL: The Athletic Institute.

Rink, J. (1985). *Teaching physical education for learning.* St. Louis, MO: Times Mirror/Mosby.

Rink, J. (1993). *Teaching physical education for learning* (2nd ed.). St. Louis, MO.: Mosby.

Strand, B., Reeder, S., Scantling, E., & Johnson, M. (1995). *Fitness education: ideas and applications for secondary schools.* Champaign, IL: Kendall/Hunt.

Vickers, J. N. (1990). *Instructional design for teaching physical activities.* Champaign, IL: Human Kinetics.

Index

Numbers followed by an *f* indicate figures.